Ninjutsu

(Ningetsu tech)

現代人の忍術

現代人の忍術：図解説明

Ninjutsu:

Illustrated and Defined for the Modern Person

or

＝忍術の現代的實用法＝

A Practical Method for Applying Ninjutsu for the Modern Person

by 伊藤銀月 Gingetsu Itoh

translation by eric shahan

ISBN-13: 978-1505216868
ISBN-10: 1505216869

現代人の忍術

伊藤銀月

※   other works in translation   ※

Sugawara Sadamoto Series

The Complete Martial Arts of Japan Volume One: Gekken
The Complete Martial Arts of Japan Volume Two: Jujutsu
The Complete Martial Arts of Japan Volume Three: Kenbu

Gingetsu Itoh Series

Ninjutsu no Gokui
Gendaijin no Ninjutsu
Ninjutsu to Yojutsu

Other Kobudo Translations

Takagi Oriemon with Robert Gray and Maurizio Mandarino
Heiho Yukan Volumes 17~20
with Kazuhiro Iida (at some point)

This is Itoh Gingetsu's final book on Ninjutsu. *Partial* reprints are available under the title 忍術極意秘伝書 *Ninjutsu Gokui Hidensho*. A full reprint of the original was published in 2002, but it is difficult to come by even at specialty shops.

Translators note:

Itoh Sensei often uses, like many Japanese authors, characters combined with parallel or, occasionally completely unrelated readings. For example, the Chinese Kanji characters read "experience" but above them the reading given is "memory". In this case both terms are describing the two aspects of the same thing. He is trying to wedge in two terms to explain one concept. Basically, in English, it looks something like this:

m e m o r y
I have no experience in/of that.

Trying to match the particles coming after it can be tricky but the effect is one that is actually somewhat common in many books and *manga* today.

Japanese also has a great many more sound words for things. In English, bees go *buzz* and a falling body goes *thud* and Wolverine's claws go *snikt*. On the other hand, Japanese has the sound of turning heads *Hyo*! the sound of boiling water *Buka Buka* and the "sound" of someone being scolded *Gami Gami*! These are kept as is, and they appear here and there in the text.

Itoh Sensei writes the word Ninja as *Ninsha* which is another reading of the characters. For the sake of the modern reader the word Ninja has been retained, however note that Itoh Sensei has used this variant reading/pronunciation.

圖解
説明

現代人の忍術

伊藤銀月著

Gendaijin no Ninjutsu

Table of Contents

III. Modern Methods for Training Ninjutsu

<u>Chapter One:</u>

The Training Undergone by Ninja of the Past was Unbelievably Severe. (First section)

◎ Method for Conducting Shūgyō in *Mu Shoku*
(Number One of the *Roku Mu*)

◎ Method for Conducting Shūgyō in *Mu Kei*, shapeless
(Number Two of the *Roku Mu*)

◎ Method for Conducting Shūgyō in *Mu Seki*, trackless
(Number Three of the *Roku Mu*)

◎ Method for Conducting *Shūgyō* in *Mu Sei*, voiceless
(Number Four of the *Roku Mu*)

◎ Method for Conducting *Shūgyō* in *Mu Soku*, breathless
(Number Five of the *Roku Mu*)

◎ Method for Conducting *Shūgyō* in *Mu Shū*, Odorless
(Number Six of the *Roku Mu*)

Chapter Two:

The Training Undergone by Ninja of the Past was Unbelievably
Severe. (Middle Section)

◎ The Art of Separating Oneself from the Mortal
   Flesh
                     (The first of the Shi-U)

◎ The Art of Self-Preservation Through Flying.
                     (The second of the Shi-U)

◎ The Art of Ascension
                     (The Third of the Shi-U)

◎ The Art of Shrinking Distance
                     (The Fourth of the Shi-U)

Chapter Three:

The Training Undergone by Ninja of the Past was Unbelievably Severe. (Last Part)

◎ *Moku Ton* Tree Escapes
(Using Trees in Order to Erase One's Presence)

◎ *Ka Ton* Fire Escapes
(Using Fire in Order to Erase One's Presence)

◎ *Do Ton* Ground Escapes
(Using Earth in Order to Erase One's Presence)

◎ *Kon Ton* Metal Escapes
(Using Metal in Order to Erase One's Presence)

◎ *Sui Ton* Water Escapes
(Using Water in Order to Erase One's Presence)

◎ The Ura Goton will only be covered in outline form

Chapter Four:

This is the Modern Ninjutsu Training Regime

Chapter Five:

The Practical Effects and Examples of *Kibun Tenkan* and *Chu-i Tenkan*

Chapter Six:

With War Seemingly Certain the Era of Ninjutsu Upon Us

Gendaijin no Ninjutsu Table of Contents

END

Gendaijin no Ninjutsu

<u>A Modern Practical Guide to Ninjutsu</u>

by Gingetsu Itoh

translation by eric shahan

A General Outline and The Responsibilities of the Author

and for the Modern Person

First off when someone mentions Ninjutsu, one is like to imagine fingers of the hand gripping in strange patterns to seal an incantation or mumbling some sort of strange verse with a *Munya-munya* mumbling sound. The result of that entwining of fingers and muttering of curses appears and an exclamation of "*Aara!* Quite mysterious!" is emitted. Now in front of your eyes a half-hearted trickster clears the smoke away and a rat the size of a horse leaps out, or a mortar–sized toad comes crawling out or a great serpent some two *Jō*[1] in length comes creeping along. In other words it is nothing but a method of mass entertainment that's hairy with sleight of hand and minor trickery. A bunch of techniques for mucking about. When brought up in conversation it is half-heard or coolly laughed off. This is the response from the average, everyday person.

Should this not be the case it is, at most, a method for manipulating small chances to pilfer money or valuables, inconsiderately taking advantage of people who have let their guard down. They strike like a wind then conceal their form. This slippery method could be seen as admirably effective, though in peoples' minds it is held in low regard. Such is a particular *Kuse*[2] of the well-educated intelligentsia.

That is the extent of the way Ninjutsu is perceived amongst both the general public and the intelligentsia. Though they may seem to be

---

[1] 丈 One Jo is 3.03 meters.
[2] 癖 Habit (good or bad). A tendency to.

differing viewpoints, in fact they are both disparaging Ninjutsu or otherwise brushing it off lightly. At the same time there is harbored an element of mystery, of nervous doubt or some feeling in between. Thus, in the end we have to admit that there is no great difference between these two standpoints.

Naturally, in the eyes of the straight-laced people in the world today there is nothing to be had from Ninjutsu. Even should one attempt to somehow revive it for these times, what possibly could be gleaned from it? In other words, Ninjutsu holds no value in the world today. It is nothing but the dregs from an ancient past. Further along these lines, is it all but impossible to find a way for Ninjutsu to capture the interest of people and cause their passions to rise?

That wraps up a group of rather difficult questions, and the author must respond to these all with a quite unequivocally "*no.*"[1]

The reason for this is that, above all, in these insecure times, getting by in the midst of this bloody, foul smelling world can't be said to not contain the possibility that one will not have to face a life threatening situation. Also, it is difficult to judge when a violent person is going to decide to pursue you. When confronted with such a situation, in the interval created by the moment one's eyes close with a *pachiri*[2], we ourselves move in and restrain the opponent's j u s t forming assault. The opponent's *Ki*[3] is broken and their inertia flummoxed. Operating with the speed of *Den-Kō Se-Ka*[4] removing oneself from the range of the opponent's ability to pursue. Following this method enables one to safely escape and stave off calamity. This is, according to the mysteries or *Gokui* of Ninjutsu, referred to as 『*Shun Kan Sa Yō*[5]』 which is and has been in practical use. Within Ninjutsu is contained the most developed form of 『*Gendai-teki Goshin Jutsu*[6]』 , namely that which we have no choice but to label *the form of protecting the body that this world has*

---

[1] Itoh Sensei uses a Kanji character of negation 否 with "no" written above it in Katakana

[2] パチリ The sound of your eyelids closing.

[3] 氣 Fighting spirit.

[4] 電光石火 Lightning speed. Electricity-Light-Rock-Fire (spark off a rock).

[5] 瞬間作用 "Using the interval of a second."

[6] 現代的護身術 "Modern day techniques for self-defense."

been waiting for. The four Kanji[1] characters of 『*Shun Kan Sa Yō*』 which is defined as the *Mabataku no Ma no Hataraki*[2], or the *operating in the interval of a blink of an eye* will be referred to frequently, and fully detailed later on, but for now I would like to entreat my readers to remember this term in advance.

If we were to say go one step further, let us add to the above stated
shape
form of the 『*Shun Kan Sa Yō*』 a similarly perfect application of a m i n d.
These mental and physical techniques will produce a significant effect against people, against society, in variety after variety of negotiation, when faced with a chance or when confronted by something strange. In the situation where one is seeking profit as well as in the situation where one is seeking safety. All this is contained, in the highest order, within the 『*Gendai-teki Shosei Jutsu*[3]』 which is comprised of techniques that can be used in our everyday lives in this modern world. It must be said
mark
that the immediate effect of these techniques are without equal.

In view of this, Ninjutsu cannot be said to be techniques for mucking about, a method for being sly or a way of cheating. If properly
shapes
employed with the forms of the 『*Gendai-teki Goshin Jutsu*』 along with
heart/will
the before mentioned engaged m i n d of 『*Gendai-teki Shosei Jutsu*』 ,
then together they are a force to be reckoned with. Whenever the need becomes apparent they can be quickly called forth and the effect will be swift. Bursting forth, almost as if leaping about, the sharp clear energy of 『*Shun Kan Sayō*』 will capture the attention of the people living in these times to a degree that will have them all nodding in agreement.

On the other hand in the unlikely event some gang, hoodlum or
shapes
some such unpleasant violent character should try and use these forms to commit violence, or a cheater, a pickpocket or a deceiver attempt to use
heart/will
the m i n d for some evil purpose, the basis of 『*Shun Kan Sayō*』 being one that requires a serious heart devoting itself to a purpose, will result, in that moment, in a feeble, half-formed technique. In other words

---

[1] 漢字 Chinese Characters.
[2] 瞬く間の働き "Operating in the interval that an eye blinks."
[3] 現代的處世術　Modern Methods for Getting By in Life/Modern Worldly Wisdom.

『*Nin no Yabure*[1]』. It must be remembered that since the distant past this has been strictly prohibited for those of all rank. I would like to heed the people of the world now to not neglect this caution. Should one not it will fall into the category of "*a little learning being a dangerous thing*[2]" resulting in great injury.

The reason the author decided to proffer this manuscript was not to intentionally burn through flowery explanations but rather enable the reader to come to grips with the general outline of this topic.

Now, just to make sure we are all on the same page, I would like to add a bit about two elements taken from amongst the variety within Ninjutsu itself, namely 『*Goshin Jutsu*』 or defensive techniques and 『*Shosei Jutsu*』 or techniques that can be applied in modern society. These two will form the core of the Ninjutsu that one should follow through with *Keiko*[3] and moreover attempt in real life situations. A fair number of actual and lively examples will be offered as proof along with the author's serious and straightforward clarification and explanation will leave no stone unturned. I make this clear promise to my readers.

That being said in order to confirm that I have placed in my readers brains certain important elements I have again pulled out the following points.

◎ 『現代的護身術 *Gendai-teki Goshin Jutsu*』

(The group of techniques that have the greatest effect with regards to defending the body)

◎ 『現代人処世術 *Gendai-teki Shosei Jutsu*』

(The group of techniques that have the greatest effect with regards to making ones way through society)

Lining them up in this fashion should enable one to remember them with greater ease.

---

[1] 忍の破れ Breaking of the Nin. Wrecking the *essence* of Ninjutsu.
[2] 生兵法は大怪我の基 "New soldiers get hurt a lot." A little learning is a dangerous thing
[3] 稽古 Training.

現代人から見た忍術の本質とその分野
On the topic of modern people taking in the true nature of Ninjutsu.

其の一
過去の忍術は廣い意味においての偵察術であった

Chapter One

In the past Ninjutsu was Considered a Form of Observation in a Very Broad Sense.

In the long since gone past, in the era when Ninjutsu was carried out for Ninjutsu's sake—in other words the era when *Ninjutsu Sha*[1] were a given, defined as the time when that mysterious, indecipherable unparalleled manner of living and method of conducting missions was a known thing—from the Sengoku Era through to the Tokugawa Era the very top was considered to be the Shogun who was bringing order to the realm[2]. Below that were several hundred lords of various import, each striving to maintain their leverage with the other realms or houses. This contest was in reality a bloody gamble that was approached with the upmost seriousness, with each side keeping their guard up. They spied and counter-spied on each other to discover what plans were being formed.

Further, those charged with this task namely the Jutsu Jutsu Sha[3] (from here on abbreviated to Ninja or Shinobi no Mono[4]) are carrying

---

[1] 忍術者 Ninjutsu practitioners, Ninja.

[2] The Onin War (1467–1477), the conflict, rooted in economic distress, is generally regarded as the onset of the Sengoku period. The Tokugawa Era is the period between 1603 to 1868 (after the Sengoku Era) where Japan was under the rule of the Tokugawa Shogunate and the country's 300 regional Daimyo.

[3] 術術者 Using the Kanji for "technique" twice giving us something like "a technician of techniques".

[4] 忍者 Itoh Sensei writes the familiar "Ninja" as *Ninsha* throughout this volume. It is actually a correct reading of the characters but I was unable to determine when or why *Ninsha* became *Ninja*. I've replaced it with

out Ninjutsu which is, using a fairly broad definition a collection of myriad types of surveillance techniques. If we were to phrase it another way, they are, in the broadest sense surveillance techniques that can be understood by *anyone* in this modern world to a fairly extensive degree.

Well then within this "broad" definition of the surveillance techniques of Ninjutsu we have Military surveillance, National Security Surveillance, Investigative Surveillance and Personnel Surveillance. In addition to this we have "state of affairs" in foreign places surveillance and state of mind surveillance all of which can be focused on a country, focused on society, focused on people or, even on a larger scale, focused on the whole world. It is having a shape or it is shapeless. All possible circumstances are included. All of the here and theres, the nears and fars, the levels up and down, and each facet is all included, boundless in its breath of investigation, yet extremely detailed despite its span.

What this comes down to is that when it comes to Ninjutsu the way things are used and the way things are carried out are *as various as they are without limit.* They are mixed and built upon and recombined. For those not accustomed to this way, there is no method for distiguishing ^{separating} them. Unlike these days however, where training in each of the fields of surveillance is separate, according to the particular need or focus, and despite the fact that modern tactics in surveillance, taken as a whole, far outstrip their predecessors, Ninjutsu in the past simply had "surveillance". In contrast to the fact that these days people conduct the same kinds of operations in a great many situations without having to mentally prepare to put their life on the line as was done in the brutal, torturous, foul smelling, awe inspiring, moreover calamitous, lawless violence of that past era. When conducting their mission Ninja must at any point or in any place must be fully aware that at any moment their life may become forfeit. And this is not even the most important thing. There is assassination. There is sniping. There is the case where, in order to proceed, one has to take a person's life. A thing that was not uncommon. The Shūgyō [1] Keiko of Ninjutsu was completely and utterly wild, violent, amazing, frightening, painful and difficult to the point of

Ninja throughout the book as Ninsha just sort of sounds funny, but that is what he wrote so I'm just letting you know.

[1] 修業 Training in an art, often strenuous and typically demanding physical and spiritual hardship. The work Keiko means training, but not in the sense of doing the same movements repeatedly without thinking. More like "active training."

being nearly unbearable. And therein lies the value^{worth} of the Ninjutsu Sha, those that forged and kneaded their bodies to overcome this. When compared to the surveillance technicians of today, one can't help but think that even armed with a ladder they would not be able to reach that level.

Be that as it may it cannot be said that Ninjutsu is not only a continuous year round system of techniques where one's life is on the line, but also that the Shūgyō of Ninjutsu involves risk to life and limb therefore, techniques to distance themselves from having to put oneself in peril came about.

Now, if we were to move one step further and look at the particular nature of the long ago Ninjutsu, which was comprised of techniques enabling one to skirt death, and compared it to the whole of investigative techniques of today, one would find several points lacking. The seriousness of blood, shed while undergoing the strenuous training needed to achieve this level was borne by only these and when compared to other varieties of similar *waza*[1] or techniques it must be understood that a particular superiority is apparent.

The speed of this is said to exceed that of the flash from the sharpened point of a blade. It resembles the highest peak, for example, Mt. Everest amongst the chain of mountains called the Himalayas.

Were Japan to line up all the surveillance techniques of the past and present world, the one that looks down upon them would be none other than Ninjutsu. It is from there that the influence of Ninjutsu extends from. It is there that the value of Ninjutsu exists and that is the place where the whole of Ninjutsu resides. The effectiveness of Ninjutsu. The feeling of Ninjutsu. In the end that is where the very source of Ninjutsu lies. The core of Ninjutsu, the eyes of Ninjutsu, the soul of Ninjutsu, the very life of Ninjutsu and the essence of Ninjutsu. For this reason, should this one point be banished Ninjutsu itself would not have come about. It is from this one point, the crucial *Kaname*[2] of Ninjutsu, namely its unregulated one thousand varieties and its ten thousand variations, that all of Ninjutsu is born from.

In addition and further, should that one point be missing, there

---

[1] 技 A technique. A method.
[2] 要 The essential points.

would be little need to search out the particular mysteries associated with it. Moreover, there would be no secret documents to make use of in these times. This is the extent to which this single point is important.

That being said, regardless of how often the virtues of it are stated, until the reasons for that crucial *Kaname* are laid out and explained one can't expect people to be nodding in understanding. Very well, then. Like a thumb jabbed right in the eye, that one point will be made perfectly clear. It is, in other words the previously mentioned 『*Shunkan Sayō.*』 If broken down more fully, the method by with Ninjutsu achieves its success it through the use of the interval it takes to blink an eye. I would like to focus our attention on this point.

Well then, at last we have come to the portion where we will discuss that decisive point of Ninjutsu, the point that contains its excellence, the 『*Shunkan Sayō.*』 The *wheres* and *whys* of this will be explained completely, in detail, correctly and openly to the satisfaction of all my dear readers. This is the place where I have to pour all my energies into a thorough breakdown.

其の二
Chapter Two
忍術の決着點は何所にあるか
Where can the Decisive Elements of Ninjutsu be Found?

As was mentioned before, we are not referring to one technique but
rather focusing on a single particular point plucked^{pulled} from where it resides,
solely within Ninjutsu. We squeeze this guy with a *gyuu* sound and,
lowering the dissection scalpel, find in what way the razor sharp flash
emitting from a single focused point can be leveraged in this modern
world. This volume on Ninjutsu seeks to settle that question. The
answer regarding that one point is, as it turns out, 『*Shunkan Sayō.*』

First of all what is 『*Shunkan Sayō*』according to the secret
mysteries of Ninjutsu? First off, as I open my mouth to begin my talk, is
an extremely rough outline and explanation.

The scene is, being unexpectedly assaulted by a villian^{bad guy}, being chased
by a person bent on violence or falling into some dangerous situation that
is difficult to extract oneself from. Possessing a body that is kept in shape
over the course of ones daily life, resulting in a light and flexible frame.
Possessing a mind^{heart/ will} that is sharp and sensitive. Taking these two and
bringing them together as one when the body is in operation. We
ourselves actually move in on the enemy and break the first wave of his
Ki[1]. Thus having smashed his initial assault the enemy's *Ki* is then
casually and unexpectedly shifted to another place or thing using
『*Kibun Tenkan.*[2]』Another possibility is using 『*Chu-i Tenkan*[3]』to
redirect an assailant's concentration to another place and causing their
head to whip around with a *hyo!*[4] Then, however that interval must be
utilized with speed equivalent to *Den-Kō-Se-Ka*, faster than the time it
takes to go *Ah!* slipping away. Evading the opponent's *Jitusu* or true
strike and striking out with a *Kyo* or a lie, the enemy wincing at this *Kyo*

---

[1] 気 Attention, focus, fighting spirit.
[2] 氣分轉換 Shifting the Ki to another place or thing.
[3] 注意転換 Shifting the concentration to another thing or place.
[4] ヒョッ Sound of a turning head (as if one's attention has been taken)

and, in that same span of a blink,[1] moving with speed out of the range of the opponent and. This is the so called 『*Shunkan Sayō*』 of Ninjutsu.

Decisively carrying out 『*Shunkan Sayō*』 will result in an effect akin to one disappearing from in front of your opponent. It will bring out the same sense of something mysterious that occurs when 『*Onshin Jutsu*[2]』 and 『*Onshin Tonkei Jutsu*[3]』 are employed.   In other words, when decidedly executed with staring with openmouthed astonishment is simply par for the course.

『隠身術 *Onshin Jutsu*   The Art of Concealing the Body』

『隠身遁形術 *Onshin Tonkei Jutsu* The Arts of Concealing the Body and Escaping』

Having revealed the secret of this particular *Gokui* or mystery, I would like to request that it be placed firmly in the brain (head) And, in the end, I would like the decisive elements of Ninjutsu as well as its excellence to be remembered. As to how the remaining varieties and variations are applied, I leave that up to the Ninjutsu path taken by each of you.

Thusly we have finally come to the part where a somewhat more extensively detailed explanation of this second section is required. First of all, when someone is approaching from the front, or in the case where someone is trying to catch up to you from behind, or perhaps someone is approaching from the side, in a sharp, smart movement of the mind (heart/will) lock eyes with a *chira!*[4]. As the proverb goes:

More so than the heart the eyes speak

Within that person's eyes-from behind the pupil something like a color, like a ray of light, floating out. A gentle thing or not. It must be

---

[1] 虚 *Kyo* is lie while 実 *Jitsu* is truth. In this case, striking at the opponent's true attack with a feint (lie).
[2] 隠身術 Techniques to Conceal the Body
[3] 隠身遁形術 Techniques to Conceal the Body and Escape. The Ton Techniques use fire, water, birds and beasts, people, etc.
[4] チラ The sound of a quick glance or look.

rapidly[1] evaluated.   In Ninjutsu this is referred to as:

気の動きを見る *Ki no Ugoki wo Miru* Seeing the movement of the *Ki*

So once the 『*Ki no Ugoki*[2]』 has been determined, immediately, in that next second, the chance that is contained in the span of time the width of a hair must be taken. Just when the opponent is *balanced on the cusp of formulating an attack and beginning their attack*, one must move in a flash and engage first, leaving no interval. The opponent's *Ki no Ugoki* has been smashed open and that breakdown continues, robbing their body of inertia.

It goes without saying that balance once lost can be regained, but focus, once broken cannot be as easily regained. It is in this place that we will find the bankrupt in the opponent's armour.

Riding the wave of that failure in order to achieve some sort of amusing diversion by toppling someone falls into the range of "*The technique of a new soldier can cause a big injury*[3]." Should one turn their back on this prohibition of Ninjutsu then you will immediately and without hesitation beckon 『*Nin no Yabure, or the failure of Ninjutsu.*』 For this reason it is reserved for specific situations only. If things fall into place, the opponent's balance will be broken and they will go ass over teakettle. At a bare minimum the failure will result in a wince. The essential point here is that you, once having caused the opponent to falter, choose a path that allows you to rapidly move away from this dangerous situation. Whether it be advancing or retreating, both options allow a reasonable degree of latitude in escaping outside the range of the opponent.

So now we come to the question of should this situation arise, how exactly then do we carry out is this method where we smash the Ki of the opponent and then take his balance with 『*Shunkan Sayō?*』 As we possess the key to this the padlock on this very problem can be opened

---

[1] 蚤く The Kanji is for "flea" which has another reading as Hayai はやい or "fast." ie. Fast as a flea can jump.
[2] 氣の動き The movement or "intent" of the Ki (spirit).
[3] 生兵法大傷 *Nama byoho ookizu.*

with a *pa-ching!*[1]

This key is something that will have an immediate visible effect. ^{indication}
Something that your opponent was born with, the operation known as:

眼の防衛本能 *Manako no Bōei Honnō,*

The Self-defensive Instinct to Blink

This reaction has been flipped around, snatched away and *put to our advantage.* The meaning of 『*Honnō*』 being the instinct we are inherently born with. A completely untaught, naturally activated ability. Within this we have the *Bōei Honnō* which activates when an unexpected danger is sensed, in the second the mind is coming to grips with the situation and completely unknown even to ourselves, rapidly causes the body to react. With a *Ha!* the hand leaps out or with a *Gyo!* the body jumps back. But here, before we go further, first understand that the clever, alert eyes move before all of this with the eyelids closing to a *Pachi!* sound at lightning speed. This reaction is the same whether you are smart or whether you are a fool.

Making use of the chance here to suppress the enemy and disentangle oneself from a difficult situation and escape is the *Kaname,* the essential point, of the 『*Bōei Honnō*』 of Ninjutsu. This slim margin within which one must act in is referred to as:

Utilizing the defensive reflex of the opponent's eyes to your advantage.

If we were to frame this in a real situation, first, as was mentioned before, the 『*Ki no Ugoki*』 must be read. Having grasped that ephemeral thing, you must launch yourself at the chance that *resides between the opponent mentally committing to an attack and actually enacting it.* Then leaving not the slightest gap startle the 『*Bōei Honnō*』 of the opponent's eyes into operation. There are two categories:

First: Techniques not using the hands and feet.

Second: Techniques using the hands and feet.

---

[1] パチン The sound of something snapping open (like a lock).

Interestingly, the reason 『Techniques not using the hands or feet』 is in first position is due to the fact that, to put it quite simply, there are more effective options available. Techniques that do not rely on the hands and feet can be done and, moreover, be enacted quickly. I think that we should place a great deal of emphasis on this last point. That being said it doesn't mean that the first one is going to be suitable in every situation and therefore in some cases the Second is going to be more appropriate. It perhaps goes without saying that as both of these will be used in a *Rin-ki-o-hen*[1] fashion, they can be viewed as being equivalent.

If we do a breakdown of 『Techniques not using the hands and feet.』 we arrive at:

◎ Glare fiercely at your opponent crushing his concentration. (This is presuming a firm grasp of how to put power into your eyes thus enabling the strength of your gaze to shrivel your opponent.)

◎ Emit a huge scream thereby forestalling the opponent's attack. (This too must be such as the very guts of the person receiving the scream have no choice but to react. One must be able to roar like a lion.)

◎ Aiming between the eyebrows, spit directly on your opponent. (Surely everyone is capable of doing this, but when we are under pressure the possibility that the mouth will dry up and we have to consider that there might not be any saliva.)

That more or less wraps up the three varieties. Within them, however, there are undoubtedly one or two that are going to work really well for some people while at the same time there are some that are not really going to work for others and should as such probably be avoided. The third one involving spitting on the other hand is one that, should they not become flustered, women or children could easily do. If carried out flawlessly in a certain situation, even a surprisingly large man can be overturned.

Well we've come again to the part where I am going to drone on a bit with my explanations. We all understand that we have these three and one is aiming at a point between the eyebrows and spitting. While not

---

[1] 臨機應變 A common Japanese expression meaning to respond to issues as they arise or "play it by ear."

hitting the eyes, of course, the 『*Bōei Honnō*』 causes the eyelids to close with a *Ha*! In contrast to this the effect of the First and Second is to shock the opponent to the level where their "guts go cold[1]." These too, of course, then can be wedged in to the realm of the "*instinctive response of the eyes*" with no real argument. Indeed it is without a doubt this part that is going to result in the most resistance from my readers. I'm not trying to make excuses here however, on a basic level as anyone can perform this Third one, I hoped to focus my readers attention upon it. As it is a technique anyone can perform it therefore differs from the First and Second. In other words I made every effort to simplify this in order to get this idea to bounce around in my readers' minds. As practical measure I chose to arrange them in a way that would result in the least likelihood of them getting entangled. Though I placed the other two above the one that can be understood at a glance, I beg your understanding. Be that as it may it is hardly a stretch to say that should someone's shriek suddenly wash over you or the scolding finger of a severe dressing down come at your face you would startle and, without any conscious thought, your eyes would shut.

Next we will take a look at 『Techniques using the hands and feet』 which have limitless methods of application. If we were to break it roughly in two it would look like this:

自物 *Ji-butsu*- Items on your person :

Using items in your hands or on your person.

他物 *Ta-butsu*-Items around you:

Making use of appropriate items around you as well as naturally occurring items.

自物 *Ji-butsu* include, but are not limited to, the following:

- ◎ A lit rolled tabacco.
- ◎ Any book, newspaper or magazine in your hand.
- ◎ Anything you may be carrying wrapped in a *Furoshiki*[2] or other style package.
- ◎ A walking stick. Either a Western or Japanese style rain

---

[1] 膽を冷やす *Kimo wo hiyasu*. Strike terror to the core.
[2] 風呂敷 A large piece of material used to wrap up things of different sizes.

umbrella or sun umbrella.
◎ A *Sensu[1]* hand fan.
◎ A portfolio, a bag with a strap, a bag hanging from your hand, a *bag[2]* or a basket.
◎ Other kinds of implements related to work or portable items.

Clearly there are other possibilities but I will stop at this sort of overview.

Moving directly to 他物 *Ta-butsu* we have:

◎ Bits of rock or gravel used for repairing or improving roads.
◎ Fallen scraps of paper, board, sticks and so on.
◎ Fence posts, flagpoles and other such nearby things.
◎ An unused wheeled cart.
◎ A hanging tree branch.
◎ Dirt, sand or clumps of soil on the ground.
◎ Other items or tools that that seem abandoned or dropped by their owners or items close at hand that if used for the interval of a few seconds would not result in any loss for its owner.

Of course there are other possibilities.

At last we are at the point where we can take these man-made objects and these natural objects and see how they can be put into play in an actual encounter. If, for example, as previously mentioned, reading the 『*Ki no Ugoki,*』 in other words the color in a person's eye, the shift of light in a person's eye, and then, as soon as you have determined that the villain intends to assault you or a violent person is intent on pursuing you, in the moment they decide to attack but before the attack is formed- neither too early nor too late as one is operating in the interval it takes the eye to blink, we launch a courageous assault from our side with a *Den-Kō Se-Ka[3]* like *speed*. Should our *waza[4]* use 自物 *Ji-butsu* then they should be immediately employed. Should they use 他物 *Ta-butsu* then they should be taken up and applied. That item or thing should be whipped like lightning right at the space where the nose meets the eyes,

---

[1] 扇子 Folding Japanese fan.
[2] バッグ Itoh Sensei uses the English word here possibly referring to a Western style bag.
[3] 電光石火 Lightning speed. Electricity-Light-Rock-Fire (spark off a rock).
[4] 業 Technique or movement.

or with a *Sa!* punch right in that spot. The inherent defensive mechanism of the eyes will activate in the opponent-this is as I previously stated, an instinctive reaction that rises unbidden- and the apparent danger of our attack will naturally be sensed by the eyes and the will blink closed with a *Pachi*! In that interval, moving precisely and sensitively, neither early nor late, direct your body with a *Pa!* sound and shift to either advance or retreat. And rapidly and easily remove yourself to a place out of harm's way. This is the 『*Shunkan Sayō*』 of Ninjutsu. To the enemy it appears that a human has simply vanished out from in front of them. This clearly indicates a similarity to 『*Onshin Concealing the Body Jutsu*』 and 『*Onshin Tonkei Concealing the body/Escaping Jutsu.*』 The way the techniques are clinched, their decisiveness and overall applicability along with the flash of light interval where the eye blinks must all be examined.

I would like to note that the technique, which falls under the heading of 『Techniques using the hands and feet』 and in the sub-category of 『自物 *Ji-butsu,*』 namely the flicking of 『A lit rolled tobacco,』 is the one that has the highest level of effectiveness. When used expertly it is in a similar vein to the 『*Ka-ton no Jutsu*[1]』 of Ninjutsu. Of course it goes without saying that one cannot simply walk about with a roll of lit tobacco in one's mouth on the off chance something might occur, so I can hardly recommend that. It is up to fate.

When speaking of techniques using 他物 *Ta-butsu,* or items around you, one example given was 『An unused wheeled cart.[2]』 This one in particular requires a completely separate explanation. It is not simply a matter of the difference between 自物 *Ji-butsu* and 他物 *Ta-butsu* but rather other objects or tools can be used as they are to enact the 『*Shunkan Sayo*』 by taking them in your hand and flinging them at the eyes of the opponent. In other words these are sort of a halfway 『Techniques using the hands and feet.』 A technique that more simply embodies the realm of 『Techniques using the hands and feet』 would be easier to digest. This so-called 『Unused wheeled cart』 technique differs

---

[1] 火遁の術 Fire escape techniques. Techniques using flame.
[2] 小型の空車 To be truthful I am not sure exactly what he is referring to. Nowadays *Kuruma* means car but at that time anything with wheels was referred to as a *Kuruma*. It seems likely Itoh Sensei is envisioning a small utility cart of some form or another.

from the rest in the sense this object requires the use of both the hands and feet. What is required here then is a method that unmistakably matches the meaning of 『Techniques using the hands and feet.』 The way it would work is first the feet are used to kick the cart into a spin slamming it violently into the legs of the attacker. Making good use of the ensuing moment of surprise immediately thrust some sort of item you are carrying into the opponent's eyes, resulting in a double application. If executed flawlessly the results can be quite impressive. That being said should one's movement or timing be off, the end can result in things going topsy-turvy with the danger flipping back upon yourself. A *Yabure*.[1]

If we boil this down, while the techniques involving a lit roll of tobacco, as well as the small abandoned cart, can be extraordinarily effective, one cannot always rely on them being readily at hand. The others, even when enacted "as ordered" like a meal, are no guarantee of success and therein lies the danger. It is difficult to put either up on a pedestal or to understand their small faults.

Also under the umbrella of 『Techniques using the hands and feet』 is the 『Spitting directly on your opponent.』 The methodology is clear and it can be done without much ado. As long as you act within the bounds of the "chance" you have created, there is no reason to doubt that it will be wholly effective. In reality there are no shortcomings in this thing we refer to as 『Shunkan Sayō.』

There is another option within the 『Techniques Using the Hands and Feet』 that I purposely did not mention before involving neither *Jibutsu* nor *Tabutsu*. It is the method of for using what you were born with:

素手 bare hands

This is not saying that dropping what you happen to be carrying and using your bare hands is always the best solution, rather it is concerning in the situation where you happen to not be carrying anything. It is perhaps best to say that:

If one's hands are unencumbered, a rapid application can be completed.

---

[1] 破れ Break. In this case "breaking (failing) of technique."

When it is all said and done this technique requires more than a little precision as we must spring into action with a *Gu!*, fully committed in the interval between when the enemy formulates their attack and enacts it. Stepping in a foot-span deeper than in the case where you are carrying something in your hand and striking out in a flash with opened five-fingers. Now the lightning flash is not at the front of the enemy's face, but rather, moving deeper it seems as if it is stabbing into the back of both eyes. As long as you did not let the enemy's 『*Ki no Ugoki*』 escape you, then a spectacular success is assured. The way the foot moves in. The way the hand lashes out. The total commitment of your attack, as well as the overall physicality of the movement, is not easy to come by. *Step in deeper than you think. Thrust out with the hand farther than you intend.* The reason for this is that the effect will be lost should your movements be too shallow. Therefore in the course of your daily life strengthening of the body and mind is essential.

In summary the 『*Shunkan Sayō*』 of Ninjutsu is carried out by startling the 『*Bōei Honnō*』 of the attacker by first catching hold of then reading the 『*Ki no Ugoki*』 that appears somewhere in their eyes. From there we cannot be satisfied simply with grasping the moment that occurs in the interval between when the enemy formulates their attack and enacts it, but must then explode out with a completely unexpected strike, riding our bravery forward. If not then, immediately, anxiety of the opponent will grip the chest, you will startle and the hands will instinctively rise up, the body will begin to form a defensive posture in conjunction with this, and everything will have gone topsy-turvey with our own innate reactions activated. And it will fail. A *Suki*[1], or opening in your guard, that you shouldn't have given the opponent. We will have to suffer a crushing defeat. Yet this is beyond simply a case of 『*Nin no Yabure,*』 but rather we must classify this as none other than a place *a thousand ten-thousand Ri*[2] distant from Ninjutsu.

To change tracks a bit, I believe that despite my proceeding gingerly though this, there are probably a great many readers who, isolated from Ninjutsu, feel that in this world we are wrapped up in, Ninjutsu, whose roots and base are in the past, cannot have anything to offer. That being

---

[1] 隙 A gap. A small fault that can be exploited.
[2] 千万里 A thousand 10,000 *Ri* (1 *Ri* = 2.44 miles). Used to refer to a vast distance.

said we cannot really answer their questions without drawing upon the Ninjutsu of the past therefore, and of course this stage was long in coming, we will look at the way Ninjutsu Sha historically learned, the way they memorized, the way they strengthened, the way they hardened their bodies and the way they carried out Ninjutsu. Through all the changes, through all the differences, through all the hardships, through all the intensity, through all the surprises, through all the fear, it is the tale of the very best being selected. Actual experiences will be lined up with true accounts and I intend to offer by degrees numerous sections containing what I believe to be interesting, yet moreover profitable examples. First though I think we should take a look at what profit can be gained from the Ninjutsu of the not so distant past.

Namely the so called   『五遁 *Goton* "Five Escapes" Jutsu[1]』 :

木遁 *Moku Ton* "Tree Escapes",

火遁 *Ka Ton* "Fire Escapes",

土遁 *Do Ton* "Ground Escapes",

金遁 *Kon Ton* "Metal Escapes",

水遁 *Sui Ton* "Water Escapes."

In addition to these five we also have the 『裏 *Ura* or "Reverse" Goton Jutsu』 :

人遁 *Jin Ton* "Human Escapes"

禽遁 *Kin Ton* "Bird Escapes"

獸遁 *Ju Ton* "Beast Escapes (*Nezumi* "Rat" Jutsu and so on)"

蟲遁 *Chu Ton* "Insect Escapes" (*Hebi* "Snake" Jutsu, *Gama*

---

[1] 五遁の術 This topic is covered in depth in the book <u>Ninjutsu no Gokui</u> by Itoh Sensei, which has also been translated.

"Toad" Jutsu, *Kumo* "Spider" Jutsu and so on)

魚遁 *Gyo Ton* "Fish Escapes"

In addition to these five varieties there is also:

霧隠れ *Kiri-gakure* "Concealing in Fog" Jutsu

and

霞隠れ *Kasumi-gakure* "Concealing in Mist" Jutsu.

Moving along down the road from this starting point there are a multitude of possibilities and variations awaiting, *a thousand possibilities and ten thousand changes[1]* of design exist. There is a bottom to this. There is a lid. In addition, like a tree, there is a trunk. There are branches. And leaves. While a full discussion of each would prove problematic, and though an abbreviated discussion would leave as many questions as it would answer, when it is all said and done it is that whisper thin decisive margin, the *Kiwamari Te[2]* that defines the preeminence of the 『*Shunkan Sayo Onshin*』 『*Tonkei Jutsu.*』 I would like to firmly place in your mind the finely sharpened point, that these fluid one hundred thousand ten thousand variations all have the power to return to a single point.

Should one be suddenly attacked or someone should leap out and seek to pursue you, when humans run into a difficulty or are faced with danger they attempt to wring every ounce of power they have out of themselves. We cannot deny that this degree of power approaches a spectacularly almost incomprehensibly fearful level. One cannot say when we will have an experience akin to the un-beckoned 『*Shukan Sayo*』 of Ninjutsu. The reality of untangling oneself from danger or escaping from trouble, whether by brave heroes from the past or done by famous gentlemen of today, will raise a cold sweat in your gripped palms as we proceed through numerous examples. However these chance encounters are not relayed simply to draw a *Hyo*! double look, but instead are intended to pose the question of whether or not, in the same

---

[1] 千變萬化 *Sen-pen-ban-ka.* A multitude of possibilities.
[2] 極まり手 The move that decides the match or bout.

situation you yourself would be able to always engage in the same way
and if not then the value of the 『*Shunkan Sayō*』 of Ninjutsu is not truly
being appreciated. In other words, if you are not able to envision this
then you have not embraced Ninjutsu. The question we must ask now is
how then can we bring Ninjutsu to the forefront?

There is no other. One must recall, should one fall into the pit of a
life or death situation, the feeling of that whisper thin chance that
is 『*Shunkan Sayō*』 coming out unbidden with a *Hyo!* One must think
back on that bit that remains, like a half forgotten dream and utterly and
completely bite into it, crush it between your teeth, and if that is done,
sometime, when the same set of circumstances arises you will not allow
the chance the width of a hair, between when the opponent formulates
his attack and engages it, to escape from you. Part of your nature is
having this at the ready, the body light and nimble, the mind sharp and
sensitive, and of course both halves operating in unison. If a chance is
felt or a changed sensed then immediately, like a fuse trailing toward and
igniting an explosive device, a technique is activated from us in the
interval of the blink of an eye, breaking the enemy's *Ki* and go so far as to
destroy their balance. This is the result of applying and layering *Kufū*[1] to
your *Keiko*, or training.

If done, then your initially rough, cobbled together 『*Shunkan
Sayō,*』 which at first is going to be nothing more than the instinctive
Hyo! of whipping your head to face the threat, will almost unnoticed
begin to knead your body and mind into shape. The 『*Shunkan Sayō*』
of Ninjutsu which is embedded in your body will begin to purify and you
will be able to respond in a time of crisis with an ingrained response like
pulling your handkerchief from your pocket. Succeed in *Rin-ki-o-hen*[2],
the sense of responding to any situation and *Hen-tsu-ji-zai*[3], the sense of
being freely adaptable. One will be able to report the success that has
come from intense Shūgyō. And even should one have no experience of
facing such a threat, properly preparing one's self through layer upon
layer of Shūgyō will certainly enable you to drill in some remembrance
that could perhaps be put into play in a real situation.

---

[1] 工夫 Tricks learned to help a technique or method to success.
[2] 臨機應變
[3] 變通自在

33

Adding a little to this as we conclude, the ultimate goal of this way of learning Ninjutsu, this way of ingraining the 『*Shunkan Sayo*』—and the related Shūgyō methods—all must be included. Primarily, 『現代的護身術 *Gendai-teki Goshin Jutsu*』 is defined as the most effective method of self-defense *Jutsu* for these times, along with its parallel 『現代的処世術 *Gendai-teki Syosei Jutsu,*』 namely the most effective way to navigate one's way through this modern society.[1] This can be surely done by anyone. While the following explanation that I have prepared will be thorough and careful, I would like to join with this examples offered as evidence of actual situations that transpired, the fierce battle for survival that took place both in the past by great and legendary heroes as well as those involving gentlemen in these days and times for your consideration. Numerous situations where techniques identical to the 『*Shunkan Sayō*』

of Ninjutsu *rose up unbidden*. I intend to bring on to the stage Kenshin Uesugi, Hideyoshi Toyotomi, Kyomasa Kato, Yukimura Sanada, Kotetsu Nagasone, Judo Saigo, Juru Hoshi, Yukio Ozaki as well as other luminaries one after the other before your very eyes.

As a sort of added bonus of sorts the author himself will present a tale from his own days as a youth.

---

[1] In the sense that you cannot be overcome by others' will. You can succeed in your enterprise.

其の三　現代的忍術の三方面

Chapter three:　The Three Divisions of Modern Day Ninjutsu

Rising above the techniques existing within other methods, Ninjutsu peaks in a steep sharp tower, energetic and vital. If the spark flashing off the top is grasped in the naked hand, and worked into the daily lives of those breathing the air in this modern world, you will find it merges perfectly. Taking this into consideration, the people of today, when compared with the era of Ninjutsu, have vastly more refined thinking, but, be that as it may, and despite the gulf of time that separates that time from us, Ninjutsu seems to have a ready-made purpose within the realities of today and, as its effectiveness will be proven, the value of it will rise with a *Gu-n!* , undoubtedly drawing the attention of those about.

Now, coming to the stage where we take a look at just where the life we have breathed into Ninjutsu can be leveraged in this modern world, note that there are three broad categories. However, as was done before in this volume the ordering and explanation of the information is going to be presented in a new way to maximize understanding.

I.　一 偵察術 *Tei-satsu Jutsu*

Reconnaissance Techniques (Finding the truth about secrets)

II.　二 護身術 *Goshin Jutsu*

Techniques for Self-Defense (Easy techniques for protecting the body)

III.　三　処世術 *Syo-sei Jutsu*

Worldly Wisdom (How to find success while making your way in the world)

It goes without saying that these three highly effective techniques for the world today are not in a rigid order. Further, we must first add the word *Gendai-teki*[1] or "modern" to the front of each word.

Having begun to seek in earnest to continue the 『*Gendai-tek*i Reconnaissance Techniques』 of Ninjutsu of the distant past we will find that it is abundant with various useful avenues. The situations where it

---

[1] 現代的 Modern or "Modernistic".

can be applied are many and, moving on from where I mentioned this
before, these new investigative techniques *march hand in hand with the
intellectual pursuits of today.* These 『Reconnaissance Techniques』 of
Ninjutsu, if joined with those available now, will steadily add to your
ability.^strength Also it goes without saying that the Shūgyō employed by the
Ninjutsu of long ago, that brutal trying frightening thing, is hardly
something that modern man seeks. That being said, bone-crushing
Shūgyō *is not necessarily warranted here either.* In the end we can just
pluck out the best of parts of Ninjutsu, namely that which is not
contained in other arts, the 『*Shunkan Sayō*』 . We can use the same
guiding principle with the 『Reconnaissance Techniques』 of Ninjutsu as
well. The 『*Gendai-tek*i Reconnaissance Techniques』 of Ninjutsu and
the value^worth attached have remained constant like a ship making for a
constant star.

Next let's look at 『*Gendai-teki* Self-Defense』 and rope off the area
that Ninjutsu covers. As was covered in the chapter dealing with
『Where can the superior points and decisive points of Ninjutsu be
found』 the *Kimari-te* or *Oku-no-te*[1] that is 『*Shunkan Sayō,*』 defined
as "operating^working in the interval of a single blink." Now, putting a little
muscle into clarifying everything from the lineage and history to its role
and the way it is used, down to how it is employed. As this is quite a span
that I hope^plan on to dissect and disseminate and as the majority of the outline
has already been introduced, for a finishing touch of sorts I plan to crown
the whole thing off with a chapter on 『Modern Training Techniques for
Ninjutsu along with Practical Modern Applications.』 I intend^plan for this
chapter to focus heavily on methods of studying, methods of learning,
methods for conducting Keiko as well as what kind of Shūgyō should be
done. Obviously placing that information here would only cause
confusion.

With regards to that I would like here to answer the question as to
why the 『*Shunkan Sayō*』 of Ninjutsu is considered the most effective
of all in a clear, decisive manner. For this I need to be completely
effective in my explanations.

---

[1] 極まりの手 *Kimari no te.* Move that decides a match or a game. 奥の手
Oku-no-te. A secret way of moving to decide a bout or a game.

Despite taking pains to avoid dangerous situations, should one be
unexpectedly be accosted by a ruffian^{bad person} or in a situation whereupon one is
suddenly pursued by a violent person, and quite rapidly you can find
yourself grappling or running about or in a *Ha-mono Zan-mai*[1]. How
then can we keep ourselves whole? In many cases you have to fight off
the attacker, injure them or risk being injured or hurt in the process.
People in the area around you could get caught up in the trouble as well
and, even should they not, know that as you are like to go crashing about
in the general area, causing a commotion. The result is always the same.
Becoming a burden to the police, causing a commotion amongst the
locals, inviting a mass of rubberneckers[2], impeding the conduct of
business for a while and, for Pete's sake, a general impediment to the
running of peoples' daily lives. One doesn't want to become a nuisance to
the country or to the people of today, so, in the end, your good
neighbours and friends are going to be deprived their due despite their
labours all due to your embarrassing situation. My oh my, not a very
intelligent[3] way to end up.

Therefore and thusly one must withdraw from that situation to a
completely different and higher realm outside of danger. Correctly
reading the 『*Ki no Ugoki*』 floating somewhere in the eyes of the
opponent in the moment they form their plan of action but before it is
enacted. Leaving no gap between the reading of this and we ourselves
engaging, smash the opponent's *Ki* in a *Den-Kō-Seki-Ka* flash of
movement, which is followed by the balance being broken and you can
make away to beyond the border where he can reach you. And, like the
lights suddenly going out in the theater, you vanish from the equation
only to reappear in a later scene cool and unruffled, the so–called
『*Shunkan Sayō*』 of Ninjutsu enabling one to escape untroubled and
painlessly-no leaving one's tail behind like a lizard to fool the enemy,
slipping away from danger with no fuss, detangling oneself from
hardship and feeling as if emerging from all of that to a clear cloudless
day. In order to get by in this unsettled, brutal, foul smelling, cruel world
the 『Self-defense』 that I have spoken of stands tall on the border of all

---

1 双物三昧 A furious fight with knives.

2 彌次馬 *Yaji-uma* or "people one after another coming to see a horse."

3 智慧 *Chi-e*. One definition for the characters can refer to the Sanskrit
word *Prajñā* meaning wisdom that is able to bring about enlightenment
(related to Buddhism).

this and no doubt its boundless value^{worth} is going to cause one to nod in agreement at its necessity.

While there is a somewhat reserved artistry to this 『Goshin Justsu』 but this is in no way the peak of Ninjutsu, but rather there is another level above this rising spectacularly higher. In answer to the question, 『Goshin Justsu』 the *physical manifestation* of 『Shunkan Sayō,』 while, raising the bar to the next level, if we were to look at applying the same method to the operation of our intent or will. When consulting with people, when negotiating with people, when being consulted, when being negotiated with or from when beginning a debate with others reaching to-here the scale of things is going to leap up with a *Gu!*-intra-country dialogue. Government level talks, economic talks, talks on diplomacy, talks on society and other negotiations and exchanges in the work of people the whole lock, stock and barrel are within its span. This level that has its shape plucked right out of it, gives the mind a strange freedom of movement with the 『Shunkan Sayō.』 What happens is that in the interval between when the opponents mind begins to engage and then activates, taking that slim chance and smash their Ki, defuse their charge. It is a strategy for being freely adaptable in any direction. Strike with a *lie* at the opponent and escape his *reality*. It is the manifestation of the operation of the myriad possibilities of *Sen-pen-ban-ka*[1]. This serves to change the blink of an eye from no advantage to an advantage and, without a doubt from an advantage to an increasingly positive position. This is abbreviated as 『Gendai-teki Shosei Jutsu.』

Look, let's just imagine for arguments sake someone were to be the possessor of an above-average sharp, sensitive mind and should that person have the 『Shunkan Sayo』 of the mind at a level *higher* than the 『Shunkan Sayo』 of the body, depending on how much Shūgyō was layered atop, the effect would be immediately apparent. It is this example which illustrates the value^{worth} of 『Gendai-teki Shosei Jutsu,』 in other words the mind working 『Shunkan Sayo』 of Ninjutsu being applied by the mind^{will} in action.

---

[1] 千變萬化 *Sen-pen-ban-ka*. A multitude of possibilities.

I would say that it is about time to wrap this section up. If we were to lay out Ninjutsu, which has come to meet us from the distant past, on the cutting board and have at it with a kitchen knife, we would find parts that can cover certain gaps in our modern world, though it must be said that there are gaps that it *cannot* cover.   It must be said that the parts that are covered are in unison with these times so perfectly as to more or less spear vertically through and out the top of the world we are in now, leaving those bits that it can't be applied to as being forgivable. Surprising as a child surpassing his or her parents, like shoots of *take no ko*[1], the power of this enables it to rise high and look down somewhat piteously upon that which is below it. This is 『*Shunkan Sayō.*』

Leading the way down this path of how best to leverage the 『*Shunkan Sayō*』(under the umbrella of 『*Onshin Tonkei Jutsu*』) of Ninjutsu and how it can be made use of and applied to the modern world, are the points the author himself has focused on. These three are, namely, 『*Gendai-teki Teisatsu Jutsu,*』 『*Gendai-teki Goshin Jutsu*』 and 『*Gendai-teki Shosei Jutsu.*』 The degree of 『*Shunkan Sayo*』 in each of the three lined up before must be separated and allotted a different value.   If we were to look at the amount of 『*Shunkan Sayo*』 embedded in first one, 『*Teisatsu Jutsu,*』 we would find we need to add just a small portion of 『*Gendai-teki*』 to it.   While there are subtleties from the Ninjutsu of old that are difficult to cast off out of hand, considering the technical progress made one cannot say that those same methods can walk alongside those of the modern day. So regrettably we are forced to admit that amongst the three varieties 『*Gendai-teki Teisatsu Jutsu*』 has probably the least ^{worth}value. Next we have the second 『*Gendai-teki Goshin Jutsu.*』 The nature of this is wholly suited to 『*Shunkan Sayo,*』 thus to this particular *variety* of Ninjutsu we can all nod in agreement as we add the three character word 『*Gendai-teki*』 to it with gusto. That being said, this 『*Goshin Justsu*』 encompasses only the ^{body}physical form and thus is difficult to say applies 『*Shunkan Sayo*』 at a level higher than all others. On top, in third position, we must recall the one that fully encompasses 『*Shunkan Sayo*』 through its operation of

---

[1] 竹の子 Bamboo shoots. This plant is famous for sending roots underground to reappear several yards away from the main plant (often in a neighbour's yard).

the mind.^{will} Of the three varieties it is this 『*Shosei Jutsu*』 of Ninjutsu that can be best leveraged in this modern world. It is this 『*Gendai-teki Shosei Jutsu,*』 that is the most effective followed by the one in second position 『*Gendai-teki Goshin Jutsu*』 and finally the one with the lowest value^{worth} 『*Gendai-teki Teisatsu Jutsu.*』 It is best to differentiate them according to their relative value.

The author's goal in releasing this manuscript to the public is to draw notice to the 『*Shunkan Sayo*』 particular only to Ninjutsu and to address the problem of how it can be best leveraged for these modern times. Simply put we are talking about raising 『*Shunkan Sayo*』 to a new level and using it to refer solely to the operation of the will. That we are then thereby placing a greater value^{worth} on 『*Gendai-teki Shosei Jutsu*』 would seem to be rather obvious.^{clear} This is, however, not the *Hondo*[1] followed by Ninjutsu, rather it should be seen as a sort of, well, separate sub-topic. The *Hondo* of Ninjutsu would probably best be described as having the 『*Shunkan Sayo*』 being of a rank equivalent to or just below that of the operation of the body, which forms the core. Thus it is 『*Gendai-teki Goshin Jutsu*』 that should be seen as being in the forefront. It is with this in mind that the author places 『*Goshin Justsu*』 on the *Omote*, or obverse and 『*Shosei Jutsu*』 on the *Ura*, or reverse giving a *Hyo-ri* or Obverse-Reverse balance[2]. Taking this duality as a central theme, I would like to fully investigate whether we can apply 『*Shunkan Sayo*』 to the whole of the modern world. Further and in addition, I would like to note that elements other than 『*Shunkan Sayo*』 will be mixed in, particularly 『*Gendai-teki Teisatsu Jutsu*』 which will alternately conceal itself and then go into hiding in a rather charming fashion. I would like to request that my readers keep this in mind as we go along.

Finally, I would like to introduce a method for comparing the two sides of the coin, the *Omote* and *Ura* that I just mentioned. That is placing above the 『*Shunkan Sayō*』 employed by the body^{form} for 『*Goshin*

---

[1] 本道 Way. Main path.

[2] 表 *Omote*-surface or obverse. 裏 *Ura*-backside or reverse. 表裏 *Hyo-ri*. When then characters are joined to mean "obverse and reverse" at the same time the reading changes to *Hyo-ri*.

Justsu,』 that which difficult for people to grasp, 『Onshin Jutsu.』 Above the 『*Shunkan Sayō*』 enacted by the mind for 『*Shosei Jutsu*』 is that thing that people cannot calculate, namely 『*Onshin Jutsu.*[1]』 But no, despite everything, more so than Ninjutsu being put to the best use in this modern world is the value of the effect, being a hundred thousand times amplified from the long ago age of Ninjutsu is certain. The haphazard nonsense that is shown as "Ninjutsu" in cheap storybooks and movies of today are clearly to be seen as foolish.

---

[1] 隱心術 The middle character of this "*Onshin Jutsu*" is heart or mind. Thus the Romanization of the term is identical but the characters this time make "Concealing the mind/heart/intention Techniques" as opposed to "Concealing the body Techniques" of "*Onshin Jutsu* 隱身術." This is likely a term created by Itoh Sensei.

其の四　現代的忍術の三原則

Chapter Four: The Three Principals of Modern Ninjutsu

Within this if there is but a single technique, there is a way it can be carried out. And it follows that if there is one path then there is always a way it can be taught. As such and moreover, if there is a method of teaching then there is always an established law directing it. The basis of that law is referred to as a *Gensoku,* or principle. The particular *Gensoku* that have come down to us from the Ninjutsu of the past are spectacular things.

Originally the main meaning of Ninjutsu was to be able to see straight through to the bottom of an adversary to their weakest point. Pulling out that s e c r e t, or, on the other hand, making off with something important to the enemy. If not then going after the *Kubi* of the *Taishō*[1]. This is nearly all the primary situations that were conducted. The seven levels are as follows:

- ◎ 引受 *Hiki-uke.* Undertaking. (Receiving and undertaking an order from a *Taishō* or superior from your own side)
- ◎ 發足 *Hossoku.* Setting out. (Setting out from your own side)
- ◎ 道行 *Michi-yuki.*　Along the trail. (Time spent in transit to your destination)
- ◎ 到着 *Tōchaku.* Arrival. (The state of having arrived at your destination)
- ◎ 仕遂　*Shitoge.* Successfully completed. (The state of having completed the task)
- ◎ 道行 *Michi-yuki.*　Along the trail. (Time spent in transit on your return)
- ◎ 引渡　Hiki-Watashi. Handing over. (The handing over of an item collected from your destination to the *Taishō* or superior from your own side. If not the case then reporting on the success of your mission)

The whole of these seven stages are within the area "roped off" by

---

[1] 首 Kubi. Means "neck." Used in the same way we say "Off with his head."(The Japanese use "Off with his neck.") 大将 Taisho. Can refer to either a military leader or some sort of boss or kingpin.

Ninjutsu, not that I am attempting to state that this is the entire scope of it, rather that this comprises eighty or ninety percent of it. Thinking of this in terms of the *Michi-yuki* of Ninjutsu the remaining ten or twenty percent are not visible on the surface....in other words it is the decisive 『*Shunkan Sayo*』 element of 『*Onshin Tonkei Jutsu*』 , the *Oku no Te*. That wraps up the report on the historic "stages" of Ninjutsu.

For the above reasons the Ninja of the past when in the process of carrying out their important matters to their conclusion, in other words down to the final seventh stage of *Hiki-Watashi*, neither their body nor their will was their own. It must be understood that attempts to earn praise or to carry out techniques to unnecessarily threaten people, conducting entertainment style displays of skill such as juggling or sleight of hand and the like, using hypnotism to play petty tricks, conjuring up mysterious things to get people to gape, along with general mischief and mucking about, in other words activities not essential to the work at hand, were seriously admonished against and prohibited.

In other words Ninjutsu was a strictly controlled, moreover a serious method designed to prevent those conducting it from straying from the correct path.

For this reason the Ninjutsu of the past was equipped with three
solemn ^{strict} underlying principles for the established laws.

一　ichi: 忍の上 *Nin no Jyō*

To stave off things dangerous with no harm unto him, no harm unto thyself, is the mark of Nin no Jyō.

二　ni:　忍の中 *Nin no Chū*

To stave off things dangerous with harm coming to him but no harm unto thyself, is the mark of Nin no Chū.

三　san:　忍の下 *Nin no Ge*

Barely escaping with harm coming to both him and thyself, is the mark of Nin no Ge.

The above being the three *Gensoku* of Ninjutsu. Simply put, should one be in the situation where you are below the third one...in other words in the situation whereupon you have to kill the opponent in order to make your escape, in that situation where no other option is available, this is referred to as 『*Nin no Yabure.*』 This is considered to be the greatest *Haji* or shame of a Ninja. "I am completely inept!" is all one would be able to hear from such a person. Someone to be mocked or pitied.

In reality not an exemplary figure. In reality not a person who operates correctly. In reality a person without deep understanding. In reality a person who is not aligned with *Dori,*[1] or reason.

In addition, one cannot look at phrases like *"To stave off things dangerous"* and consider the movement used be any other than the 『*Shunkan Sayo*』 of 『*Onshin Jutsu.*』 Further looking at not causing injury to your opponent, this must include even not inflicting any bad recollections on the opponent while not allowing the same injuries or difficult memories upon yourself. 『*Shunkan Sayō*』 allows one to leave with no entanglements, to efficiently and cleverly carry out your 『*Onshin Jutsu,*』 stave off danger with a calm, cool expression. This being done by that rare, exceptional breed that conducts Ninjutsu at the highest level, those whose status was designated long ago in the past, those with 『*...the mark of Nin no Jyō.*』 The author writes with vigor regarding taking this 『*Shunkan Sayō*』 and leveraging it for use in 『*Gendai-teki Goshin Jutsu,*』 and I must repeat this is neither some fool's errand or some self-centered theory, nor is it something that is designed to suit only myself but rather it is a real thing that can be relied on, a point that cannot be disputed. To put this plainly, even should you not allow any injury to befall yourself, if your opponent is injured then we have, well, already sunk to the realm of 『*...the mark of Nin no Chū*』 and all sense of the upper echelon of Ninjutsu has been lost.

To consider this more in depth, let us first lay eyes on the situation where we have injured the opponent. Suddenly the situation goes haywire, getting flipped around so that up becomes down. In other words we will have gotten ourselves in a situation where escaping will not be a true "escape" and one will inevitably end up cornered. Next we have to consider the case where both you and the opponent are injured and in pain. You have probably already determined that

---

[1] 道理 Way + Logic.

44

Ah, this is clearly in line with one dropping down to the lowest strata, thereby becoming 『Nin no Ge.

It is unlikely that many are now not nodding decisively in agreement.

The *Gensoku*, the principle, states 『To stave off things dangerous with no harm unto him, no harm unto thyself, is the mark of *Nin no Jyō*』 is perfectly matched to the 『*Shunkan Sayō*』 of 『*Gendai-teki Goshin Jutsu*』 and, whether we look at it from the perspective of *Dōri*[1], or from the perspective of something to be practically used, we again end up with a thing leaping up to incomparable heights of superiority and we have no choice but to stamp our approval with a Taiko Drum sized *Hanko*[2].

What this all comes down to is the three *Gensoku* determined by Ninjutsu of the past, that which we are now taking the time to bring back from the dead, namely the 『*Shunkan Sayo*』 of 『*Onshin Jutsu*』 that forms the base of 『*Gendai-teki Goshin Justsu*』 will, as we breathe more and more life into it, clearly return to its original status. In short, the three *Gensoku* of Ninjutsu that remain to us from days long past, are not some sort of empty husk that is just lying about, but rather something that, if taken up and leveraged properly as Ninjutsu for these modern times, will result in a thing that has a value that far exceeds the worth it contained in that long past time.

---

[1] 道理 Truth, reason. The way things have progressed and are connected up until now.
[2] 太鼓判 Taikoban. A seal-stamp the size of a Japanese style drum. A metaphor for unconditional approval.

其の五　　忍術は高級なる兵法及び武術と合致す

Chapter Five:

Ninjutsu is both a high caliber art of war as well as a fighting style.

As was previously mentioned, deciphered and expanded upon, it must be understood that Ninjutsu has, when referring to it's 『*Onshin Tonkei Jutsu*』 of 『*Shunkan Sayo,*』 what no other system or *Gyōhō* has, namely this point, that when plucked out rises far above all else. Something that is unhindered, something that does not hinder. Something untouchable, something that does not touch. Something that is not violated something that does not violate. Whether in light or in dark it suffers not. Neither clouds nor fog obscure it. The feeling is like a winged horse kicking to the sky, whose thoughts and movement become one in *Jiyū-jizai[1]*. Things having hair and the like, skin and the like, flesh and the like, tendons and the like, organs and the like attached to it are all *completely* ground and stripped away by Ninjutsu. Moreover having torn off or peeled off these things the true *Aji[2]* of what remains will naturally begin to reveal its true value, and most people inhabiting the word we are in now will find a highly superior system of fundamentals and techniques related to the arts of war and martial arts. The brightness of these two pillars is such that they are not likely to soon dissipate.

The principle of the art of war...in other words, thoroughly investigating the source for the *Dōri* containing methods of warring, that god-like thing that warriors of today still revere, that thing that the Chinese Military Scholar Sonbu authored, the book titled <u>Sun Tzu</u>[3]. It

---

[1] 自由自在 Free and unrestricted movement. To be in complete control.
[2] 味 The flavor of, the sense of something.
[3] <u>The Art of War</u>. The military strategy treatise by Sun Tzu (known in Japanese as Sonbu or Son Shi 孫子), probably written sometime after 771 BCE containing thirteen chapters, each of which deals with a different aspect of warfare. Widely known, it has"...for the last two thousand years it remained the most important military treatise in Asia, where even the common people knew it by name."(SAWYER, RALPH D. <u>The Seven Military Classics of Ancient China.</u> New York: Basic Books. 2007. p. 149.)

admonishes that,

> *Even should a person fight a hundred battles and win a hundred battles, true virtue will not be the result. To cause soldiers to yield without fighting is the mark of true virtue.*

That the essential points of Ninjutsu should be in *complete* unison with the ideas in this text is both mysterious and profound.

In other words the 『*Shunkan Sayō*』 of which we speak is mobilized and the leading edge of the opponent's *Ki* is broken, his initial attack thwarted, and, after their attack has been formulated but before it has been carried out, in midst of their feet and hands not yet being engaged but on the cusp, that chance is grasped and, in that interval of a second your life is preserved through advancing or retreating. With this rapidly disengaging yourself from danger and escaping from trouble. Further no remnant of trouble is left behind, and this is not some story tacked onto the end but rather the *Oku no Te* of 『*Onshin Tonkei Jutsu*』 which links directly to and completely comprises the passage 『*To cause soldiers to yield without fighting…*』.

Let's try it another way. If we take what we have learned from the *Three Gensoku* of Ninjutsu then, 『*To stave off things dangerous with no harm unto him, no harm unto thyself, is the mark of Nin no Jyō*』 is equivalent to 『*To cause soldiers to yield without fighting is the mark of true virtue,*』 while 『*To stave off things dangerous with harm coming to him but no harm unto thyself, are those that become Nin no Chū*』 lines up with 『*Even should a person fight a hundred battles and win a hundred battles, true virtue will not be the result.*』 Dropping down somewhat we have 『*Barely escaping with harm coming to both him and thyself, is the mark of Nin no Ge*』 which we have no choice but to assign something along the lines of 『*Fighting a hundred battles and winning fifty,*』 I feel it is very interesting that Sun Tzu's Art of War and the *Three Gensoku* of Ninjutsu line up like fitting split *Wari-bashi* back together[1].

---

[1] 割り箸 Wooden chopsticks passed out at restaurants that are still partially attached to each other. They break quite cleanly (usually) so have become a metaphor for "two halves of a whole."

There is another famous line by Sun Tzu which means roughly 『*The odds of winning are irrelevant, only fight if you must.*』 The numerous naval battles won by the Saint-Admiral Tōgō Heihachirō[1] can serve as proof in that regard. Hmm... but even more than that, we need to look at how this marches *perfectly* in unison with the 『*Shunkan Sayō*』 of Ninjutsu and commit that fact to memory. In other words, in the span of time where the enemy has not engaged his attack, rapidly reading the 『*Ki no Ugoki*』 in the color of their eyes and launching an attack from this side without leaving the slightest interval. Not waiting for the battle to begin to start exchanging blows but rather the difference factor between which side is going to win and which side is going to lose can be said to have been previously ordained. To say nothing of Ninjutsu's 『*Shunkan Sayo,*』 that thing that is put to use in 『*Gendai-teki Goshin Justsu,*』 which in the span shorter than the width of a hair before battle begins is where you operate, in that moment rapidly manipulating the opponent's weakness in that moment. We can marvel at the notion that this example nearly surpasses the words of Sun Tzu. In addition, again drawing on the words of Sun Tzu, we have 『One who makes many calculations wins, one who makes few calculations is defeated.』 Here the meaning of "calculations" is evaluating the enemy, the enemy evaluating our own forces and the relative thoroughness or relative incompleteness of preparations of each. If one thinks of successful

---

[1] 東郷 平八郎 Marshal-Admiral of the Navy Marquis Tōgō Heihachirō, (1848 1934), one of Japan's greatest naval heroes, eventually "*sainted*" as a *Shinto Kami*. Early successes included the sinking of a British transport ship involved with ferrying Chinese troops in 1894 (He also became famous for deftly avoiding a diplomatic conflict by pointing out that the British ship had been ferrying hundreds of Chinese soldiers towards Korea, and these soldiers had mutinied and taken over the ship upon the appearance of the Japanese ships) and cumulating with the destruction of the Russian Baltic Fleet at the battle of Tsushima in 1905. Having "... broken the Russian strength in East Asia, and is said to have triggered various uprisings in the Russian Navy (1905 uprisings in Vladivostok and the Battleship Potemkin uprising), contributing to the Russian Revolution of 1905. "He was termed by Western journalists as "the Nelson of the East", after Horatio Nelson, the British admiral who defeated the French and Spanish at Trafalgar.   Wikipedia.

application of 『Shunkan Sayo』 as being represented by these "many calculations" and conversely an uncertain outcome being represented by "few calculations" there will be no confusion.

It is not limited to this either, the 『Shunkan Sayō』 of Ninjutsu with its observing of the opponent's 『Ki no Ugoki,』 the smashing of the leading edge of their *Ki* and disabling of their initial attack seeks out the 『Is knowing when a chance has arrived understanding the divine?』 of Sun Tzu. This spectacularly pierced directly through the middle of it, does it not? Snatching that nearly ephemeral chance and, leaving not the slightest gap, completely break down the enemy with the *Den-Kō-Se-Ka* application of *Waza*. We have no choice but to state that this is approaching a t r u l y spiritual level of movement. If we were to summarize all this then the pinnacle of Ninjutsu, when compared to the height of that supreme art of war, is found to be the same. This serves to show its coincidence with the highest echelons.

At the same time this applies to Kendo and Judo as well as others such as with *Yari* the Japanese spear, with *Naginata* the Japanese halberd, with the 鎖鎌 *Kusari-Gama* chain and sickle, with 十手 *Jutte*, with the 棒 *Bō* staff, with the 鉄扇 *Tessen* metal fan, and indeed all those famous experts in the martial arts develop and store sufficient spiritual power. It goes without saying that vigorous training in strengthening the *Ki* is done, and by means of this, before the body can be moved, in the interval where the hands and feet have not yet begun to move, pressure is rapidly applied to the enemy, causing them to bend, causing them to become completely immobilized as if bound hand and foot. Standing there as if petrified. If not this then smashing the *Ki* of the opponent, causing the enemy's balance to be broken and, much like someone that has had their bones removed, become gelatinous and as a slug doused with vinegar moving with a *Guniya-guniya*. In other words this leverages the meaning of 『The odds of winning are irrelevant, only fight if you must』 along with using 『To cause soldiers to yield without fighting...』 as is. This is all being said by some ironic guy doing a fine jig like two boys playing tug o war with a dust rag.

忍道 Nindō- The Way of Nin

From the very beginning those that seek the path of Nin, are on the Ki-Dō the other path, the strange path. Not on the Sei-Dō, the true path.

However, that notwithstanding, it is not a kind of strange path moving away From righteousness, it is not an "other" path without truth.

It must be thought of as a unification of the true way with the unconventional. In the end it cannot be pulled apart from the path of righteousness. A strange pulled away from the true it is not. Should one wish to separate the strange from the true, that person will always fall onto the path of evil, their body will fail. This is undoubtedly what is known as Nin no Yabure,

Decidedly a caution and one that cannot be ignored. Become one with the essence of Nin, by following these short phrases and nothing more. 有 U, the state of "is" becomes 無 Mu the state of "nothingness." And, 無 Mu becomes 有 U. 実 Jitsu, or reality, becomes 虚 Kyo, or a lie.

And, turn 虚 Kyo into 実 Jitsu. In other words, 有-無-虚-実 U-Mu-Kyo-Jitsu are in constant flux. Through this you can begin with Mushoku-Mukei, or colorless and without shape. You can become expert at Musei-Museki, or voiceless and trackless.

You can reach an understanding of Musho-Muki, or without smell and without Ki. With this you will be one with 天地 Ten-Chi, the Heaven and Earth. This is known as the 六無 Roku-Mu.

The Way of Nin is no more than this. The manner in which this is to be done is to first move toward the others eye. Yet following this you no longer register in their eyes.

However be that as it may, one is already in the middle of another's pair of eyes, somewhere under heaven and earth. And the avoiding of these is the great subtlety of becoming Ten Chi. Simply put it is resting the body above the eyelashes of another.

One method for avoiding the eyes of another is through this.

Your eyelashes being, in other words, a thing that you yourself cannot see. While the flame of a standing lantern can be said to penetrate the darkness of night. One must remember that the base of it is shrouded in darkness.

The saying that "at the base of a lighthouse ten thousand soldiers can be hidden," no doubt follows this theory. If you are able to snatch up that flitting, split-second flash of a chance. The fate that will befall the opponent is to be broken a hundred times. And be defeated a hundred times.

Zen practitioners should learn from this and take the Bokatsu[1] to disciples with weak concentration. Sword masters should learn from this and cut a swath through any rapids set to come their way. Further, Ninja should learn from this. And, when appropriate, rapidly shift the body as to the scale of a fly's eyelash. The fly's eyelash refers to fighting in the space above the eyebrows. And it is there the enemy is destroyed.

Those on the path of study, please activate of your own accord your own powers To search yourself deeply for Kufu that lie within yourself.

This is not something that needs to be awaited, like the ending to a long story. Rather the place this invention emanates from is already there.

Ninja[2] expertly move in out and through the 天地人 Ten-Chi-Jin and expertly shift between the self and a thing. These are called the 遁形 Tonkei Techiques. Tonkei is, in other words, causing a thing becomes your self and your self becomes a thing.

---

[1] 棒喝 A method used by masters of Zen (or martial arts) of scolding practitioners by either shouting at them *Katsu,* or striking them with a scolding stick, a *Bokatsu.* The Chinese master Linji Yixuan (?–866), wrote in the 臨済録 *Rinzai-roku* (Chinese: *Línjì-lù*) or *Record of Linji*:

> *A monk asked, "What is the basic meaning of Buddhism?" The Master gave a shout. The monk bowed low. The Master said, "This fine monk is the kind who's worth talking to!"*

[2] Here it is actually written as "Ninja." WTF?

What is up and what is down becomes inverted. In and out exchange places. There is a transference[1] between U 有 and Mu 無. Pure truth and falsehood are laid in opposite positions and by these means avoid the eyes of others. For this reason it is known as the Tenkan conversion between the Kyo-Jitsu of truth and falsehood.

---

[1] Transference: Transference is a phenomenon characterized by unconscious redirection of feelings from one person to another. an act, process, or instance of transferring

Day Moon Star Cloud Fog Thunder Lightning Wind Rain Snow. These are the ten Heaven Escapes.

日遁、月遁、星遁、雲遁、霧遁、雷遁、電遁、風遁、雨遁、雪遁、是れ天の十。

Ni Ton, Ge Ton, Sei Ton, Un Ton, Mu Ton, Rai Ton, Den Ton, Fu Ton, U Ton, Setsu Ton, Kore Tenno Jyu

Tree Grass Fire Smoke Earth Roof Metal Stone Water Steam. These are the ten Earth Escapes

木遁、草遁、火遁、煙遁、土遁、屋遁、金遁、石遁、水遁、湯遁、是れ地の十。

Moku Ton, So Ton, Ka Ton, En Ton, Do Ton, Oku Ton, Kon Ton, Seki Ton, Sui Ton, Yu Ton, Kore Chino Jyu

Man Woman Old Young Rich Poor Bird Beast Insect Fish. These are the ten Human Escapes.

男遁、女遁、老遁、幼遁、貴遁、賤遁、禽遁、獣遁、虫遁、魚遁、是れ人の十。

Nan Ton, Nyo Ton, Ro Ton, Yo Ton, Ki Ton, Sen Ton, Kin Ton, Jyu Ton, Chu Ton, Gyo Ton, Kore Jinno Jyu

In addition, when all is hazy around, there is no fog. So if it is taught then that on the outside of this there lays a hazy fog. Through this one will be enlightened to the meaning of the Ten Ton "Heaven Escapes,"

In the midst of darkness step on white. Thinking it is water and it is stone. Converting that stone to water, understand that the stone is transformed water. And through this we can be enlightened to the meaning of the Chi Ton "Ground Escapes."

Through oneself become another and should one be able to effortlessly become oneself through another. Then the thread connected to the ideal of Jin Ton "Human Escapes." Can be said to have been grasped firmly.

Further, with regards to the Go Ton "Five Escapes," they must be adhered to as with the Tonkei. Moku, Ka, Do, Kon and Sui. Which are modeled after the Tree, Fire, Earth, Metal and Water of the Go Gyo[1].The theory behind each being balanced evenly notwithstanding, there is a difference in the Do-Sei[2] stillness and movement of each. Moku and Do are about becoming silent. In every sense we, through this becoming Moku-Do "Tree-Earth." And should we, through Moku- Do become our self, no matter what the place or how strange it be, those still with breath in their bodies seek.

Fire and water are things of movement. A spark off a stone flying into the eye. In the interval the surface of the water is struc. Only the something we have become is seen. Deftly the lively movement of a flash of lightning is seized.

And though this is a life or death situation, it is miraculously turned to fortune. For us it is like playing in a parallel Ten-Chi "heaven and earth." In other words the manifestation of calmness and relaxedness,

---

[1] 五行 The five elements in Chinese Philosophy. Known as *Wu Xing* in Chinese.
[2] 動静 State of either stillness or movement. Overall condition or state.

Finally know that Kon is a combination of the two states of Do-Sei. To be one with the way of Nin, it is essential you train and strengthen the combined body and mind. Possessing a fierce bravery and a commitment to diligent labour. All are essentials.

And the reason for this is that you live in an eternal cycle of facing extreme danger. Something that can be said to subtly and completely fill all of Heaven and Earth. Becoming as clear as the blood red sun of morning in the sky.

Should you be unable to see truly, then nothing will appear in the midst of your field of vision. In order to follow the Sei "correct" path of Nin, you must become akin to the strange, differing of "Ki." Those now on the path of learning should take this to heart.

Even when broken down into modern Japanese this *Kanbun*[1] appears quite scraggly and has an old musky odor about it emanating with a *Gotsu-gotsu*. I have every intention of attempting to clarify the maze-like phrases but, as the passage is particularly brutal and should too many of the words be replaced with more accessible ones, then the whole thing is like to fall apart. At the same time I desire to protect the teeth of the modern reader so that they do not crack apart in frustration this torturous passage. Having gone over the text once and joining that with bits and pieces of explanation by the author, I believe that times when you are nodding with understanding will not be infrequent. That being said, while the pace is somewhat leisurely, proceeding on with a *Botsu-botsu*, here and there while unraveling the dense maze we will come across points that discuss the nature of what Ninjutsu is. It is hard to say that in those places new discoveries will not be unearthed. Primarily though, we will focus our attentions on Ninjutsu and the arts of war and military strategy and how each of these parts meshes to the

---

[1] 漢文 Text written entirely in Chinese characters (without native Japanese Kana) and utilizing Chinese word order. Originally most documents were written in this fashion with small symbols written along the sides of the text to help indicate where Japanese particles go and to show word order changes. *Kanbun* poems can be found today on many monuments, headstones and so forth, and is taught in schools (primarily High School and University) similar to how Shakespearian English would be taught. I was unable to locate the source of this particular Kanbun. (If you do, please let me know!)

other with a perfect *Pi-tari!* sound as they fit together. Rest assured that the placing of the text of *Nindō* has not been an exercise in futility.

Throughout the text in question there are more than a few sections that come across as complete gibberish, therefore I am obliged to add a bit of commentary to these sections to avoid you thinking ill of me. Namely the line 『*Simply put it is resting the body above the eyelashes of another, Through this there is one method for avoiding the eyes of another,*』 along with the rather confusing 『*Further, Ninja should learn from this and, when appropriate, rapidly shift the body as to the scale of a fly's eyelash. The fly's eyelash refers to fighting in the space above the eyebrows and killing the enemy there.*』 In reality these rather strange and decidedly bizarre verses seem to be referring to something not in a metaphorical sense. As it turns out the explanation of this is not as difficult as was previously implied.

First of all the worst thing one can do is to try and move away from the opponent's immediate surroundings. Pulling away from the enemy will only draw their attention more fully, and you will undoubtedly become classified as a target in their eyes. If one does not escape to some place then there is a real danger that a standoff will ensue. Therefore, you should do the opposite. Conversely, to put distance between yourself and the enemy one must first completely commit to a burst of action that will startle the enemy. Approaching the opponent with your own body as if attempting to drive directly into the center of the enemy's body. No, "approach" is too loose a term. Making your body akin to a musket ball is preferable, and with that speed blast open a hole in the center of the enemy's torso such that the inertia of you flying forward carries you straight through to the enemy's back.

Taking a look at 『eyelash,』 this is in other words referring to *Matsuge*[1]. *Matsuge* can be seen by another person, but they cannot be seen by their owner. To put it simply, the meaning is that *they are too close to be seen*, and this point is, in other words, what we need to grasp. Snatching up that split-second interval between when the enemy is deciding on an attack and actually engaging that attack and without any loss of time launch an offensive from our side. Using the previously

---

[1] 睫毛 Itoh Sensei uses both the word 睫毛 *Shomo* and 睫毛 *Matsuge* to refer to eyelashes. The characters are the same but the word *Matsuge* is far more common than the former.

mentioned explosion of speed and inertia, fly in at the opponent. At the same time the enemy's *Ki* is smashed, we have moved in so close as to have become like *Matsuge* and thus all but unseen. That we *no longer register in the field of vision of those bewildered eyes* is the meaning of what was being described. As for what is next, either the hand or something being held by the hand is shot out or whipped around and the baffled enemy's eyes, confusing and startling them. When the body senses danger and blinks, the readiness of the upper body essentially begins to crumble. For a brief moment, something like a day-dream like state will ensue, if not a flustered state of confusion. When it is all said in done the enemy will be completely broken. Without losing that sliver of a moment, we can next, at last, set about our original goal: separating ourselves from the enemy. As the chance presents itself we rapidly move into action and applying the same rapid flying movement, the 『*Shunkan Sayō*』 of 『*Onshin Tonkei*』 which will enable us to register a spectacular success. In all ways we have erased our presence from the eyes of the enemy and, further, it must be said that without much difficulty we opened a great deal of distance between ourselves and the enemy.

Next we run into 『*Rapidly shift the body as to the scale of a fly's eyelash*』 which contains two characters that start with *Mushi-hen[1]*. So what strange thing does this decidedly strange word, pronounced *Meishō*, refer to? It is a metaphor for an insect so unbelievably small that it cannot even be seen. Vast numbers of these bugs can rest even on the eyebrows of a fly, all the while battling it out with each other in a murderous free-for-all.

Describing something with outrageous exaggeration and purposely using ambiguous wording seems like something Soushi[2] would do. That

---

[1] 虫 Kanji characters that have the character for "bug" on the left-hand side. Frequently indicating the Kanji itself is the name of a bug.

[2] 莊子(Chinese: Zhuangzi). Approximate dates of birth and death 369-286 BCE. A Chinese philosopher active during the Warring States Period. Author of the philosophical text Zhuangzi, which is skeptical, arguing that life is limited and knowledge to be gained is unlimited. The term 無為自然 Mui-Shizen or "abandoning artifice and just being oneself." Zhuangzi was renowned for his brilliant wordplay and use of parables to convey messages. Such as:

is not to say that Ninja of the past were wont to brag and boast, but rather, in reality they were armed with the fact that no one other than a Ninja could comprehend it.

We~ll, I suppose I will just leave it at that.

魚之樂   The Happiness of Fish

Zhuangzi and Huizi were strolling along the dam of the Hao Waterfall when Zhuangzi said, *"See how the minnows come out and dart around where they please! That's what fish really enjoy!"*
Huizi said, *"You're not a fish — how do you know what fish enjoy?"*
Zhuangzi said, *"You're not me, so how do you know I don't know what fish enjoy?"*
Huizi said, *"I'm not you, so I certainly don't know what you know. On the other hand, you're certainly not a fish — so that still proves you don't know what fish enjoy!"*
Zhuangzi said, *"Let's go back to your original question, please. You asked me how I know what fish enjoy — so you already knew I knew it when you asked the question. I know it by standing here beside the Hao."*
The Complete Works of Chuang Tzu. Burton Watson. Columbia Univ. Press 1968:188-9)

忍術の現代的練習法及び現代的實用法

Modern Methods for Training Ninjutsu and

Practical Modern Applications

其の一　　古への忍者の練習法は餘酷烈過ぎた(上)

Chapter One: The Training Undergone by Ninja of the Past was Unbelievably Severe. (First section)

At long last we have arrived at the section whereupon the author will undertake his greatest responsibility, namely detailing the methods by which Ninjutsu was learned and studied, or the way of Shūgyō if you will. The way in which *Keiko* was conducted will be described to the readers in such a way as to enable anyone who wishes to be able to follow such training. If it is all right with you I am ready to get started.

The core of the learning being sought by people of the world today is a combination of 『*Gendai-teki Goshin Jutsu,*』 or the most widely applicable techniques of self-defense, along with 『*Gendai-teki Shosei Jutsu,*』 or the most widely applicable techniques for making one's way in the world. All we need to add to this are some of the dregs of that long ago Ninjutsu, that somewhat musty junk we must now pile up on our shoulders and drag out. We need to establish what exactly Ninjutsu was like during that era and, at the same time, not attempt to form some sort of outline but rather draw a clear border between the Ninjutsu of *Now* and the Ninjutsu of *Then*. We need to determine in what way the Ninjutsu of *Then* be connected to the Ninjutsu of *Now*. We need to decide which elements of the Ninjutsu of *Then* we are going to imbed in the Ninjutsu of *Now*. Before we get into that however, we cannot say we do not need to conduct a general investigation into what the Ninjutsu of *Then* was like. This will involve a lot of discussion focused on the Sengoku and Tokugawa Bakufu Era, yet as numerous curious facts will emerge undoubtedly your interest will be aroused.[1]

There is really nothing in today's society to compare to the

---

[1] 戦国時代　*Sengoku Jidai.* Generally considered to be 1467-1568. 徳川幕府 Tokugawa Bakufu. The period under the Edo Shogunate, 1603-1867.

absolutely and completely brutal training in Ninjutsu undergone by the Ninja long ago. Understand that is was aakin to a painful, stressful, spectacular and terrifying method of Shūgyō. Up until now, in the history of mankind, whether speaking of the past or present, east or west, nothing similar has ever existed in human history[1]. Contrary to the present, in the past the severe *Nan-gyō-ku-gyō*[2], or penance, endured by dedicated Zen monks and *Baramon* from India.[3] That this incredibly severe training can be endured is quite startling, and clearly heads must be bowed to this pure dedication, this complete casting off of the desires prone to humans. I do not believe we will not be able to set aside our interest as we peruse these passages.

If we were to take the investigators of today as an example, as they carry out their tasks they can hardly be said to be taking their lives in their hands with every job. "Detective" is a profession whereupon one can work without having to be prepared to make the ultimate sacrifice. Undoubtedly there are numerous such jobs. For the "Detectives" of long ago, namely the Ninja, this selfsame commitment was, above all, the most essential element. In that unstructured, violent, brutal, foul smelling world one is stepping into enemy territory or an area controlled by another country and evaluating the situation there, making off with important maps, documents or other such relevant items, even, get this, using deft technique to make off with the head of a Taisho or the situation where one is attempting to assassinate the Daimyo of another land. When it is all said and done one cannot reasonably expect to return from such a task still living. In other words, Ninja, the detectives of the past, *upon exiting the gate of their compound must next pass through barriers of calamity and disaster set up a hundred deep, a thousand deep.* So then, taking your life in your hands you go. Always on guard. Overcoming a multitude of obstacles and overcoming even the *Ataka no Seki*[4]. Keep in mind that until then the duty of the Ninja cannot be

---

[1] 古今東西 *Kokon Tozai.* All ages and all places. Characters are "old-now-east-west."

[2] 難行苦行 Voluntarily undergoing hardship for self-improvement.

[3] 婆羅門 A religious sect in India. Brahmins were engaged in attaining the highest spiritual knowledge by disciplining the body and mind.

[4] 安宅関 Ataka-no-seki checkpoint. Located in present day Ishikawa Prefecture In 1187 Minamoto no Yoshitsune had returned victorious from the battle of Heike and defeated the Taira Clan, yet later had aroused anger of his brother, the Shogun Minamoto no Yoritomo, who ordered that he be hunted down. Yoshitsune decided to flee with his retainers

considered to have been completed. It is for this reason the daily Shūgyō done by the Ninja long ago was approached, first and foremost, with a seriousness that reflected how it was a matter of life or death. It was of course because of this they found work for the various princes and lords, received a hereditary stipend generation after generation. It goes without saying then that having committed one's life to one's lord and master by becoming a retainer, not undergoing Shūgyō for the purpose of fulfilling your duty until your bones turn to powder, not pouring your heart and should in it would be considered a breach of that contract.

Thus we can se the Shūgyō of the Ninja of the past had to be a torturous, brutal path. There was no choice other than it be an extreme *Nan-Gyo-Ku-Gyo*. Completing Shūgyō in these six categories starting with the character "Mu," was considered to be the E, Ro, Ha or ABC's of the long ago Ninja. These six varieties/six levels of Shūgyō were used to develop and enhance those abilities that the body was born with, namely the 『Instinctive Reaction.』 And should these selfsame skills not be present in a person, it is hard to say that they would be able to enter the realm where Ninjutsu is learned and taught. This is how it has always been.

Further it must be said that the order of these 『Roku Mu』 is such that moving from one level to the next results in progressively more difficult methods of Shūgyō. In other words, when comparing the first 『Mu Shoku』 to the last 『Mu Sho』 one must be prepared to endure a *Nan-Gyo-Ku-Gyo* path which is six degrees harder.

Well then, let us break these down in the order listed above.

---

including the legendary warrior Benkei. They disguised themselves as Buddhist monks in order to cross the Ataka checkpoint, however the gateman at the checkpoint saw through their disguises. He was either touched by Benkei's courage and loyalty towards Yoshitsune or deceived by his quick thinking and clever acting or some combination of the two. At any rate in the end they were allowed to go and not turned over to the Shogun.
The Kabuki Play "Kanjincho" and the Noh Play "Ataka" both deal with this situation.

◎無色の修業法　（六無の一）

Method for conducting Shūgyō in Mu Shoku

(Number One of the Roku Mu)

This is the one in first position of the 『*Roku Mu*』 a method which is essential when one finds it necessary to eliminate the color of one's body. "The color of one's body" refers to more than just the shape of a person that can easily draw the eyes of others. It goes without saying that Ninja seek, on a daily basis, to avoid any sort of oily sheen on the skin or face, or have any part of their body polished that would reflect light. Further, to avoid appearing pale or having a pasty countenance that would draw attention, diet and exercise were carefully attended to in order to avoid these oils.^(fats) In addition in order that the face and body maintain a light brown complexion and avoid a polished appearance, a specific daily regimen of washing and way of drying the face was done. It is said that should the situation arise, a technique involving applying a thin coating of soot to the body and face was used.

Also we have something similar to the 『Hiding in the Eyelashes』, whereupon we hide the eyes behind the *Matsuge*. For example I you are born with eyes that have a distinctive brightness, particularly in order to keep that burning^(flickering) from being visible to those around you, the result of daily training would be, in cases of extreme need aside, they would seem hazy and vacant. This is shutting up the brightness of the eyes deep within the pupil.

And should the time come where one must carry out a task, the things one affixes to the body from shirts to under dressings, *obi*, leg coverings, even should one be wearing a *Tattsuke Bakama*[1] all would be dyed with a Suho[2] coloring. These are *Kufu* crafted from experiences in^(rememberances)

---

[1] 裁着袴 A type of men's Hakama that is tight fitting from the knees on down. Used by Bushi when travelling as well as by shopkeepers. Nowadays can be seen on the 呼び出し *Yobidashi* (guys who announce next bout) at Sumo tournaments. Also known as an 伊賀袴 Iga Bakama.

[2] 蘇枋 also written:蘇芳 or 蘇方. Known as Sappanwood or Judas tree dye.

the field, passed down to generation after generation of Ninja, there is a
worth
value in both the theory and the *Majinai*.[1] In other words one cannot say
that jet-black or blue-ish black or dark mouse-brown, really none of these
colors, blend and melt into the darkness of night. Regardless of how
black the night, sharp eyes can't help but pick these colors out.
Conversely, soaking material several times in a soup made up of the Suho
tree, and finished off with a final dousing in black gives us a deep red that
merges perfectly with the shadowy darkness.   Be that as it may, in
certain situations, having your body swathed in darkness, completely
eliminating all color, can result in the head to appear as if disembodied
floating there quiet distractingly. Here, however, we are untroubled as
amount the items carried by Nina is the *Sanshaku Tenugui*, which is, of
course, dyed with Suho red. This is rapidly deployed, covering the head
finishing
and face, completing the joining of the head and body in 「Mu Shoku.」

Suho, in addition, can be used as a way to clear poisons from water.
This is not saying that researchers today have analyzed and isolated the
element in Suho that blocks poison[2], but the long ago Ninja confirmed
this usage through trial and error in the field and relied on this
rememberance
experience. Above all I believe this technique to be effective. No, I am of
the firm belief that those who were the Ninja in the distant past were
extremely thorough and sealed up all possible cracks and crevices in their

---

A common export product in 17th Century Japan. It is effective as an
anti-bacterial and an anti-coagulant.

[1] 禁厭 The word Itoh Sensei uses here is *Majinai* which refers to a prayer
against illness or disaster. Traditionally incanted to protect farmers
against damage by animals or insects.

[2] FYI: *"The ethanolic extracts of forty Thai medicinal plants and three
preparations used for antidiarrheal treatment in Thai traditional medicine
were judged according to their antibacterial activity against
five Salmonella species. Surprisingly, only six plants showed antibacterial
activity against these five species. Caesalpinia sappan wood extract exhibited
the highest antibacterial activity against all isolated Salmonella strains. The
uses of the results were discussed and continued review for product
development as antidiarrheal drugs is being considered."*
From: <u>Antibacterial activity of Thai medicinal plants against five Salmonella species
isolated from diarrheal broilers.</u> Planta Medica 2012; p78 Ketpanyapong , et al.

technique where water could conceivably leak out.

Certainly there were times when Ninja were forced into a ferocious state of activity whereupon the threat becomes dry to the point of being unbearable. Enclosed in inky darkness and in the midst of not knowing whether the water you came upon is good or bad, one can use the Suho dyed *Tenugui* to draw water in. The Suho dye will serve to neutralize any poisons in the water.

In addition, whether it be the Tsuka of the Katana, or the Saya, all the various items on one's person, all the items of the Ninja are along these same lines. All are these items can then melt into the color of night, therefore and thusly, the person that is the Ninja themselves is being made to vanish. Cleary this can belong nowhere else other than 「*Mu Shoku*」 under the 「*Roku Mu.*」

◎無形の修行法（六無の二）

Method for conducting *Shūgyō* in Mu Kei, shapeless.

(Number Two of the Roku Mu)

Next in the second position we have 『Mu Kei』 which is one level more troublesome than 『Mu Shoku.』 As this is a method for eliminating the shape, it cannot be done without building upon the foundation created by the elimination of color. Keeping this last point in mind, and in answer to the question what exactly is meant by the "shape on top of color that has been taken away". The answer is that it is simply movement that, *in the midst of darkness one appears as if one is a separate and silent darkness.* The relationship can be best illustrated as in contrast to 『*Sei* 静 "stillness"』 there is 『*Dō* 動 "movement."』 Unfortunately, in order to get a firm grasp of this relationship we have to go through a slightly troublesome explanation.

The first thing we must do is recall the expressions 『*Kurayami no Ushi* "Black Cow in the Darkness"[1]』 and 『*Yamiyo no Karasu* "Crow in the Darkness."[2]』 If you were to consider these carefully, I think you would not be unable to come to terms with what is meant by the somewhat ambiguous 『Mu Kei』 in Ninjutsu. Were you to interpret 『Kurayami no Ushi』 and 『Yamiyo no Karasu』 as art, whether on paper or silk the entire sheet would be nothing but a sea of dark *Sumi*[3] ink. Of course in this situation the cow's entire body is painted completely black and is truly a black cow. Also, neither should the cow go "*Mou!*" nor should the crow squawk "*Ga!*" as both must be completely *Mu-Gon-Mu-Sei*[4] in this case. So then, how do we go about determining if it is a cow, or determining if it is a crow? The answer is in their movement. The cow walks, or, at the very least, moves its ears and tail. The crow flies, or at the very least hops between branches. Thus, though the artworks we painted are of the same *Sumi* color, within the unmoving blackness of night, the black color of the moving animals is included.

---

[1] 黒闇の牛 A black cow at night. Used as a metaphor for something hard to distinguish.

[2] 闇夜の鴉 Similar to the above, something indistinct like a crow in darkness.

[3] 墨 The black charcoal based ink used by Japanese calligraphers.

[4] 無言無声 Wordless and voiceless.

Even should you be unable to distinguish that color, one must understand that the thing is in fact there and that, in the end, the cow is a cow and the crow is a crow, and the shape of each is known. Thus when it is all said and done, if the cow does not move and the crow does not squawk, we are left being unable to determine either shape that lies before us.

The theory of Ninjutsu's 『*Mu Kei*』is that simply using 『*Mu Shoku*』in order to melt one's color into the surrounding darkness while moving about recklessly will quickly bring disaster down upon you, as that movement will instantly fix people's attention. That being said, if one cannot move then one cannot work. Therefore we have a subtle problem before us. What must be done in the end is, *when moving to hardly move at all*. This is, well, frankly, rather difficult, but with layer after layer of Shūgyō it is not impossible.

In other words, in a night so still nothing but a *Sheeen*[1] can be heard in the air. The movement of a person's body walking is transferred, and the air around moves as if a person five *Shaku*[2] tall has just gone by. And, as one moves from place to place it follows then that movement sends the air out around it allowing the shape of something to be sensed. The primary consideration while walking is to move the air around you as little as possible. It is this aspect of Shūgyō on which we must focus. This uses a kind of streamlined style of walking, no, maybe its best described as a 『*Uo Gata Method of Walking*[3]』.

What this is exactly relates to how normally one walks facing forward, with the widest part of the body making contact with the oncoming air. This will of course result in a lot of air connecting with the body and similarly the movement of the atmosphere around you being particularly large. Further, there is a lot of spring to the body here, and moreover the impact of the foot on the ground is strong. This energy rebounds from the earth and returns to the body, which increases the spring, causing the interactions with the surrounding air to increase dramatically. This is sure to give ones shape away even in the midst of darkness, and therefore should not be done. To avoid this issue, first of all turn the body sideways. With the armpit facing forward, the first step

---

[1] シーン The sound of a silent place.
[2] 尺 One Shaku is about 30.3 cm.
[3] 魚型の歩き方 Uo Gata Aruki Kata. Walking in a way that recalls a fish.

is like the character *Dai* 大, proceeding with the thighs spread wide[1]. If you were looking for some comparison then, let's see...ok like a sideways crab walk. The next position makes the legs much like the character[2] "X." The second step proceeds with the legs completely crossed. Next is the same as the first step, with the thighs open, followed, of course, by the X shape and the crossed legs again. Continuing to repeat this pattern again and again allows us to proceed in a *Yoko-Ayumi*[3]. Here the focus is on the hips, which are kept loose with the feeling of the center of the body being placed on top of them.

That wraps up the 『*Uo Gata* Method of Walking』, which serves, in other words, to minimize the amount of your body that is in contact with the air, while at the same time allowing the air to move past you smoothly. This enabling of the air to slip by you smoothly can clearly also be referred to as 『Streamlined Walking』. This method of walking lessens the impact of air, reducing the movement of air around you. While this is a bit contrary to normal thought, one can't help but nod in understanding at its effectiveness. It doesn't stop at this either. The feet are place lightly, with minimal impact upon the ground and as the body moves through the air it does not bound excessively. While at first the movement may seem foreign, as one becomes used to it a greater understanding of its effectiveness will become apparent and one will begin to grasp that it is truly only this method of walking that will achieve such results.

Should one become expert in this style of walking then one will be able to proceed lightly, flexibly and with a *Suru-suru*[4] smoothness. Note that contrary to the regular style of walking the body is overall lower in stance, and as one becomes accustomed to it, your effect on the air around you will diminish. This act will proportionally diminish the degree to which your *Katachi* or shape can be distinguished not only achieving a state of 『Mu Kei』 but also as less than half the width of the body is facing forward one can navigate atop walls, fences, hedges and

---

[1] 大 Is the character meaning "big" and is said to resemble a human figure with arms and legs spread out.
[2] Itoh Sensei writes the letter X with the Japanese phonetic pronunciation of エッキス "ekkisu."
[3] 横歩み The same characters and meaning as the more familiar 横歩き Yoko Aruki.
[4] スルスル Sound of something sliding effortlessly.

the like as if you were a spider or a slug with *Pittari*[1]-like accuracy. Further, in the narrow spaces between buildings, dense growths of trees, clusters of boulders, piles of wood, bales of rice, bales of charcoal or any items that are stacked around one can slip in and out with the *Suru-suru* sliding of a snake or a centipede, unobstructed. All in all there are numerous point where 『Mu Kei』 can add to your successes.

Another positive aspect is that while doing this *Yoko Aruki* one hand is tuck out in front as you proceed. Even should there be some obstruction in your way, it is going to make contact with your hand first, therefore no matter how deep the darkness of night may be, one needn't be concerned about cracking one's nose or forehead against anything with a *Bu!*. In addition, as the feet are moving sideways, there is no fear of catching the toe and tripping. There is another thing I wish to add here as we discuss *Yoko Aruki*. The Ninja technique of 『*Haya Aruki Hō*[2]』 or method for walking quickly, would enable anyone who tries it to achieve a walking pace whereupon ten paces are equivalent to twelve or thirteen paces of normal stride. With practice one can increase this ration to fourteen or fifteen strides without any undue hardship. The reasoning behind this is that, contrary to regular walking the thighs are spread wider. Naturally this is based on something achievable by the human body.

Further, there are other things to be gained from a certain *Yoko Aruki* Shūgyō but as this will be discussed in the chapter on 『*Mu Sei*』 , or voiceless, I will refrain from detailing it here and instead present an illustration on what we have been discussing.

---

[1] ピッタリ The sound of something fitting perfectly, like a lid to a box or, in this case, like an insect to a surface.
[2] 早歩き法 Fast walking method.

◎ Diagram of Ninjutsu Yoko Aruki ◎

Diagram Number Two (left)   Diagram Number One (right)

◎ 圖 の き 歩 横 術 忍 ◎

圖 二 第   圖 一 第

最初の一歩に股を開いた姿勢。右の手は眞直に前方へ突き出し、左の手では刀の鍔元を握つてゐる。第二を過ぎた第三歩は復びこの姿勢に戻る。

第二の一歩に脚をぶツちがへた姿勢。左右の手は前の形を少しも崩さぬまゝにす。第三の一歩は復び最初の一歩を繰返し、第四に至つてこの姿勢に戻る。

The second step shows the legs in a crossed position. Ensure the left and right hands do not change. The third step will repeat again the first, while the fourth will return to this position. The first step shows the position with the thighs spread. The right hand is stuck out straight ahead. The left hand is gripping the sword below the *Tsuba*. After the second, the third step returns to this position again.

Of course *Yoko Aruki* cannot be defined as the whole of the Shūgyō method for 『Mu Kei.』 Should a light be shone upon you while one is moving about at night, it is about relying on the shadows cast by that illumination to become like a toad, sinking into the utter stillness of a stone. Or one could be akin to a flying squirrel[1] and flatten oneself against the ground. In the case where it is more of a middle distance, as the beam of light cuts our way through the darkness, weave your way to the border where the light ends and darkness begins. Should you be walking in daylight and sense something from the nearby darkness, or striding in an area that is a blend of various patterns of light and dark intertwined, recall that which was written in 『Nindō』 namely that 『*at the base of a lighthouse ten thousand soldiers can be hidden*』 Taking this theory and applying it, when the light is strong, then the shadows cast by it are correspondingly deep. Even the slightest depression in the ground can be relied upon, as one makes their body like a weasel and flexibly stretches out to hide. All of these must be seen as, and are effective Shūgyō of 『*Mu Kei.*』

---

[1] 鼯鼠 *Musasabi*. Yeah, so that's the Kanji for flying squirrel. Good luck remembering that one. It is such a rare character that I could only find a *picture* of the foirst part of it (the second Kanji is Nezumi, or rat) it and not one that can be entered on the keyboard.

◎無跡の修行法（六無の三）
Method for Conducting Shūgyō in Mu Seki, Trackless

(Number Three of the Roku Mu)

So then, the one that is in the third position, 『*Mu Seki*』 is also clearly defined by the Kanji used. This Shūgyō was used by Ninja to leave no trace of their comings and goings, entering and exiting when observing the enemy. This is not, however, solely about being like some kind of phantom and not leaving a single track behind, but rather Ninja divided up 『*Mu Seki,*』 into three varieties all associated with the title above. They are: Even should a clear print be left behind, whether it's a footprint or some other kind of print cannot be determined. Another possibility is: Even if it can be determined it is a footprint, it is difficult to determine whether it is a human print or the print of something other than a human. Finally: Certainly a human print can be confirmed, but a determination of whether it is coming or whether it is going cannot be reached. These all fall under the auspices of 『*Mu Seki.*』 If we were to look closely at the situation where no tracks are left behind:

Walking across a grassy field or through other kinds of grasses.

- ◎ Crossing from branch to branch between trees.
- ◎ Walking from one rooftop to the next rooftop.
- ◎ Walking along the top of a fence.
- ◎ Moving along a stone fence.
- ◎ Using the fingers and toes to grasp the ceiling rafters and cross above a space.
- ◎ Alternating between walking and leaping between the corners of paving stones, or across the spine of ornamental rocks and from the top of one *Ishi tō rō*[1] to another and another.

---

[1] 石燈籠 Standing lantern made of stone. Originally imported from China used only in Buddhist temples, where they lined and illuminated paths (20 or 30 in a row is not uncommon) as an offering to Buddha. In modern gardens they have a purely ornamental function and are laid along paths, near water or next to a building. In their complete, original form (some of its elements may be either missing or additions), the five elements of Buddhism are included. The base, touching the ground, represents 地 *chi*, the earth; the next section represents 水 *sui*, or

Of course there are others but, well, I think you have gotten an approximation of what this consists of. Taking a look at any of the ones mentioned on the previous page, you won't find any mention of leaving no footprints for the entire way. To be sure, not leaving footprints behind over considerable distances can be done in order to befuddle people, but this is not something that can be accomplished by average people. We have to look to the rigorous physical training done by the Ninja long ago to find the answer to this. Taking a look at the situation whereupon a falling rain has stopped, even stepping on the edge of a stone carelessly will easily leave a muddy Waraji[1] sandal imprint. As needed a clump of thick grass or a flat stone can be utilized to remove this mud. This sort of caution is of course not something that typically concerns your average person.

Next we have leaving a footprint, not by accident but rather a sort of ironic method for confusing the enemy. This is, in other words, referred to as 『*Yuseki no Museki,*[2]』 or "leaving a trace that is no trace." This is sure to inspire a whole new kind of interest.

一 The situation where there is a footprint, but *what kind of footprint* cannot be determined.

二 The situation whereupon it can be determined it is indeed a footprint, however it is difficult to determine whether it is a human print or the print of something other than a human.

三 The situation where a human footprint can be confirmed with certainty, but a whether it is coming or whether it is going cannot be determined.

Within these three, the first 一(1) is simply jumping, jumping leaving only a small imprint therefore when looked at, is that three marks

---

water; 火 *ka* or fire, is represented by the section encasing the lantern's light or flame, while 風 *fū* (air) and 空 *kū* (void) are represented by the last two sections, top-most and pointing towards the sky. The segments express the idea that after death our physical bodies will go back to their original, elemental form.

[1] 草鞋 Woven straw sandal.
[2] 有跡の無跡

for toes? Or is that four? Or is it five? One thinks, "Ive got it!" and determines its one big one. It is more or less about making people look foolish in their confusion. Saying you don't understand? Well, that probably is the case. Saying it's mysterious? Well, if there is no other choice than it be mysterious. These are of course certainly not the traces left by a passing human, rather the problem lies with the fact that it is not feet that are doing the walking but traces left by a kind of walking done by something other than feet. In reality, it is the print left by walking on ones hands[1].

Revealing the trick of a magician may well eliminate all the mystery, however understand that this is not moving about by sticking the palms on the ground, rather only the fingertips are pressed into the ground as you walk inverted. ^{as if fallen} One has to wonder about the level of conditioning done to achieve this level of strength. We are not even talking about using five fingers exclusively. Sometimes four are stuck out. Sometimes three are stuck out. Of course this will cause any examination to become confused, and all will be struck by the mysteriousness of it. Along the way there would be larger marks mixed into the trail causing an even more conflicted reading. Upon hearing that a teasing mark in the ground is actually from a closed fist, they would probably be less surprised at coming upon a scene of cannibalism. Be that as it may this is for the

Itoh Sensei uses the delightfully archaic term 鯱鉾立ち Shachi Hoko Dachi. The Shachi Hoko, which can also refer to a killer whale, is, in this case referring to a mythical beast with the head of a tiger and the body of a carp, often pictured with the head down and body up (as if doing a handstand). It was believed that this animal could cause the rain to fall, and as such, temples and castles were often adorned with roof ornaments crafted in the form of a Shachi Hoko, as a protection from fire.

most part stepping on the edges of grassy areas or stones, moving from branch to branch of trees and then, in the intervening area, instead of the feet switching to the hands and crossing that section. Clearly this is not proposing crossing vast stretches in such a manner.

So then, next we have the situations that deal with 二(2). Here we are moving atop grasses and stones, on fences and on rooftops or walking along stone fences. As we move along jumping from stone to stone, mud or soil is left behind. As it is just that same mud and dirt scraped off by *something*, continuing at one point, stopping the next. Well, certainly this can be determined to be *some sort* of footprint, but as these marks have not formed a complete print, nothing can really be determined by them. Looking at this a little closer we realize that we cannot rely solely on confidence in our feet and their ability to leave tracks or not. To cover this uncertainty clearly one can just walk about on their heels or toes and leave no distinguishable track.

Wrapping up 一 and 二 we have to note that there is not a huge difference between there being a track yet not, therefore putting this under the 『Mu Seki』 Shūgyō of Ninjutsu is not unreasonable. Well then we have arrived at 三(3) whereupon a clear human footprint has been confirmed, and with it we have firmly placed it within 『Mu Seki』 . The reason this is a clear candidate for 『Mu Seki』 is somewhat ironic in nature though we cannot say that it is not far better associated than 一(1).

What is being said here is that while a human print has been determined, a separation cannot be made whether it indicates someone is coming or whether someone is going. In other words, what do they mean? This cannot be answered without saying that 『Mu Seki』 tends make fools of people to a greater or lesser degree. But can this almost comical foolishness actually occur in real life? Actually, it is because it is possible that it has found its place here. But let us recall here that though 『Yoko Aruki』 under 『Mu Kei』 had a considerably wide range of applications, it has shamelessly stuck its head into the territory occupied by 『Mu Seki』 which is no doubt testimony to its desire for a sweeping victory. Now at long last let us give over to a sweeping away any confusion that may remain, leaving us with, well, a simply clarity that defies expectations. 『*Yoko Aruki*』 is defined as: 『*Yoko Aruki*』 the feet are of course facing sideways, in other words facing neither forward nor back, the direction they come from or are going cannot in any way be even vaguely determined. "Quite right, as it has been laid out up to this point, with no gaps one can see it is exceedingly plausible." Going? Coming? Which path did they disappear down? There is nothing by which a determination can be made. Further, even should there be some distinguishable footprints to be had, they are so few as to be the same as there being none at all. In other words there seems to be a rather ironic feel to this 『Trackless.』 The Ninja of the past came up with a rather good idea. The progression from 『Yoko Aruki』 to 『Mu Seki』 is quite extraordinary. While this is hardly all there is, and I intend to expand and augment on it but that will have to wait until another chapter.

○忍者が歩んだ跡を晦ます三様式の圖解

（一）
足の跡か何の跡か全く判らぬ場合

（二）
足の跡とだけは判つても人間の跡か何の跡か判別し難い場合

（三）
人間の足跡とは認められても往つた跡か来た跡か見割められれぬ場合

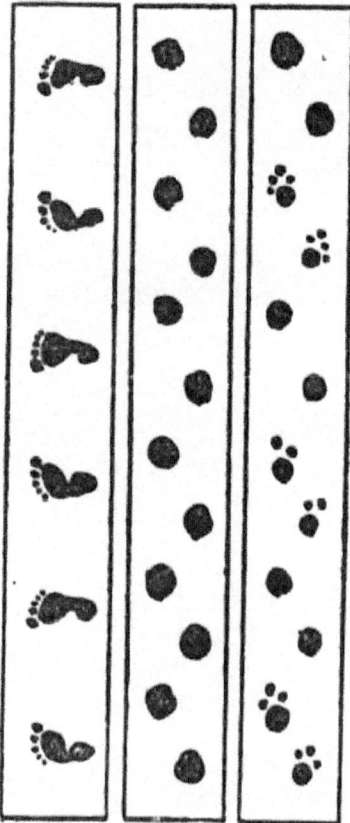

◎

Explanatory diagram of the three methods by which Ninja conceal their footprints while walking.

—

The situation where there is a footprint, but *what kind of footprint* cannot be determined.

二

The situation whereupon it can be determined it is indeed a footprint, however it is difficult to determine whether it is a human print or the print of something other than a human

三

The situation where a human footprint can be confirmed with certainty, but a whether it is coming or whether it is going cannot be determined.

76

無聲の修業法（六無の四）

Method for conducting *Shūgyō* in *Mu Sei*, voiceless.

(*Roku Mu* number four)

Next we will look at the one in fourth position, 『*Mu Sei*.』 We will find that the methods of Shūgyō become more and more difficult, to the level bones will start to be broken. This 『*Mu Sei*』 is not referring to eliminating the voice emitted from the mouth but rather an elimination of echoes or reverberations. Why then does this 『*Mu Sei*』 which deals with elimination of sound and elimination of reverberating echoes have a name that refers to vocal production? The answer resides within the desire of long past Ninja to keep the true meaning of the techniques from being revealed to the uninitiated. Their desire for secrecy was unparalleled.

It goes without saying that Ninja would not, in the course of their work, go about making vocalizations, thus giving themselves away. No matter what the situation their bodies don't make a cutting sound as they move through the air, nor is their labored breathing to be heard like some rank amateur or child fooling around. This issue has already been cut at the root, but there is still one extremely difficult area that remains. No matter where you are or how you walk, there is a Waza for eliminating the sound of your footfalls as well as their ensuing vibration. There are of course myriad conditions that can be problematic, but the list below will illustrate a few of them.

◎ Going across a pile of dried leaves will result in a *Gasa-gasa*, rustling sound.
◎ Stepping on *Shimo-bashira* or frost columns will cause a *Sara-sara,* crackling sound.
◎ If you were to walk across a frozen road a *Mishi-mishi* creaking sound will echo out.

◎ Crossing across a ^{w e a k} vulnerable bridge or *Dobu-ita*[1] gives off a *Gishi-gishi* squeaking sound.

◎ Of course stepping on a Tatami straw mat will give off a *Mishi-mishi* echo, while going down the hall will give off a *Gishi-gishi*. A hall constructed with Nightingale floors[2] are going to present some problems.

◎ In the northern areas the cold snows will sound a *Kichi-kichi* crunching.

◎ Walking down a rained upon road will cause a *Pisya-pisha*. Areas where puddles have formed will splash with a *Pasha-pasha* .

◎ A gravel road will give off a *Zaku-zaku* grating sound, while a sandy road will emit a *Saku-saku*, sliding sound.

◎ A stone road will echo with a *Kotsu-kotsu* clopping sound, while a wooden path will echo with a knocking *Boku-boku*.

◎ If the wooden cover to a hole is trodden upon it will sound a *Gotori* will sound, while if a stone cover to a hole is stepped upon a *Kotori* will be emitted.

◎ If travelling through a tunnel then a *U-wan* will echo, while going across a *Kake-hashi*, or suspension bridge will echo *Zushin*.

◎ A slippery downward slope will go *Ku-sha*, while a muddy one goes *Gu-sha*.

Allowing no sound to escape, permitting no vibration to

---

[1]溷板 *Dobu-ita*. The wooden boards that cover the ubiquitous drainage ditches lining roads. Now most often covered with concrete slabs. Typically written 溝板, with the first Kanji referring to "ditch," Itoh Sensei switched the first character out to mean "muddy," so a "muddy ditch cover" is sort of what he was intending. Yeah, it kind of took me a while to work that out.

[2] 鶯張り Uguisu-bari or Nightingale floors (actually the Japanese Bush Warbler) , are floors designed to make a squeaking or chirping sound when walked upon. Found in the hallways of some temples and palaces, the most famous example being Nijo Castle, in Kyoto. These floors were designed so that the flooring nails rubbed against clamp, causing sound to emit as the nail rubs against the other metal piece. Manaka *Unsui* Sensei Kancho of the Jinenkan stated once that, *"The floor can be overcome by rolling out your obi down the hall and then walking on that. It will serve to dissipate your weight."*

emanate. Though your step may touch the earth on the path you are taking, it is equivalent to no step having been placed. The most improbable phalanx of obstacles and barriers lie in wait on the ground, things a normal person wouldn't concern themselves with, something even the most unencumbered lay about would be unable to conjure up. Well then is what the Ninja do all that improbable? All the *Kasari-kasari* rustling, all the *Mishiri-gishiri* slogging through mud, none of these can be said to not present a serious challenge. If even the slightest bit were to enter the ears of the enemy then it would be over. The work of the Ninja would be broken apart or it would rapidly draw out into a scene where the thread of one's life would be in danger of being cut. We also have to contend with those whose ears are sharper than that of humans, the enemy's guard dogs' howl fixing upon you that wretched^{torturous} sight would be more than we can imagine here. Having gone through all it takes to clear the span from 『*Mu Shoku*』 to 『*Mu Kei*,』 followed by completing the grade in 『*Mu Seki*』 all as if following the *Ton Ton* beat of a drum, not coming away with 『Mu Sei』 one would sort of feel as if you had fallen into an artless dead end. First and foremost this shameful state leave a Ninja with his head hanging quite low indeed. If 『*Mu Shoku*,』 『*Mu Kei*』 and 『*Mu Seki*,』 from the lower ranks are not given life in 『*Mu Seki*』 then the true working nature^{quality} cannot be thought of as being there.

So then the Shūgyō for this 『*Mu Sei*』 deals one at a time with a multitude of situations wherein each sound and vibration must be eliminated by *Kufū,* or tricks you develop for a certain cituation. While this may be obvious, of greater import is viewing this as a whole as if from above and recognize that no matter what the scenario the sound of the feet and the vibrations given off by them must be muted from both man and dog. With this as a base you must train and strengthen yourself. I believe that, first of all, it is this point which must be clearly understood and adhered to.

In reality the Ninja of long ago, went to great lengths to develop *Kufū,* were decidedly intent on their pursuit, long complicated procedures were not disagreeable. A spectacularly unparalleled unique method of Shūgyō. Before we get started though, in a house of Ninjutsu, a boy child is born. At last he ventures from two-legged beast to the age

where he is a two legged animal[1].   In other words, he has gone from
crawling around and crawling around to graduating to grabbing things to
stand up. If fortunate he will manifest some indication of his bloodline,
and should that ^{innate} inherent ability become apparent, then while the child is
still unaware of how things work, the child is fooled. On top of the
Tatami mats two pieces of dampened *Tōshi*[2] paper layered together are
affixed to the floor. The parent takes the child's hand and they are made
to skillfully totter across the paper. Now this *Tōshi* paper is an imported
type of stationary usually of a brown mousy color and somewhat fragile.
This particular Shūgyō I speak of is more or less from the Tokugawa
Bakufu[3] Era. Compared with the *Tōshi* my readers and myself are
familiar with today it was considerably more durable. Be that as it may
Tōshi paper is *Tōshi* paper, so much like today it was crap, and prone to
fraying. So it doesn't really matter that it was stronger, a *Ōban*[4] coin
would likely slice through it and I can't imagine how much stronger two
pieces placed atop one another would be. Soaking it then laying it on top
of Tatami is out of the question. All things being equal, even leaving it
like that will undoubtedly result in it tearing.

   At any rate, at first the father would take the child's hand and he
would walk doubtfully with a *Tekuri-tekuri* wobble across the
aforementioned *Tōshi*. The result of these uncertain steps would be that
the shape of the feet would be imprinted; the pattern of the Tatami mat
underneath would be clearly visible. In the end, the result is that as
confidence increases little by little with multiple repetitions, the single-
minded attention to the task results in the *birth of a natural operation*.
The nerves and muscles on the soles of the feet become trained, and a
change of sorts begins to be seen. The end result is that several hundred
or several thousand sheets of *Tōshi* are lost to all this, though it is
conceivable some were repaired then layered on top again to be
dampened again. And to show just how impressive this kind of learning
can be, now no matter how many times the child walks over the paper,

[1] Itoh Sensei writes 日本足 Ni-hon ashi "Japanese Legs", which is a play
on 二本足 Ni-hon Ashi "two legs." Seems to be some sort of joke but I
don't get it.
[2] 唐紙 Also read as Kara Kami. Paper from China or resembling such.
[3] 徳川幕府 1600 until 1868.
[4] 大版 Also written 大判. The somewhat large ovular gold coins used as
currency from around 1588 onward.

the *Tōshi* doesn't rip. The next step being to remove one layer of *Tōshi* and, of course, walk him across the wet paper. Having done this, the doubled layer, which was unbroken, is now a single layer. This single layer of course will not support the previous level of conditioning, so everything virtually returns to the first stage, where the paper is ripped and pulped to pieces with a *Botsuri-botsuri* sound. What follows is again a long patient training. Tens of repetitions. Hundreds of repetitions. At last, in the end, the child unconsciously, over the course of this playtime activity, mysteriously begins to be able to walk over a single dampened sheet of *Tōshi* without it tearing. This is in other words an indication that he has graduated with highest honors. Thus from an extremely young age the muscles on the bottom of the feet are conditioned and improved. The nerves one is born with are switched to a new set of operations and the goal of the Ninja parent has been achieved. This Shūgyō done in order to build a foundation can proceed faster or slower depending upon the ability of the person in question, but it is said that typically two to three years would be required.

Originally, and this probably goes without saying, Ninja in the past did not go about building a foundation through Shūgyō without any teacher. Amongst Ninja there was in fact a social status and these *Iegara*[1] Families—in other words if you were not the house of the *Kashira-bun*[2] or head, then it was unlikely you could do as you pleased. The *Kashira-bun* would be beholden only to the *Kashira-bun's* lord or prince. Moreover, as he was more likely than not receiving a regular stipend, this allowed a lifestyle that covered more than the basic necessities, unlike the case of the former. So for the novice Ninja on the bottom end of the chain, meeting their basic needs was their first priority. Clearly the reality was that they were not as bound by obligation to a liege lord as the *Kashira-bun* was, and unless they were particularly motivated they would hardly devote the long hours and days necessary to achieve success in this.

Thus the Shūgyō required to build a base in Ninjutsu was more or less finished at an extremely young age. Once formed, in order that no cracks or vibrations affected it, daily *Keiko* was engaged in the field so that regardless of where one walked, naturally no sound or vibration

---

[1] 家柄 Good family, family of pedigree.
[2] 頭分 Kashira-bun. Lit "head" or boss.

would be emitted. Completion of this rigorous physical conditioning of the child was the responsibly bore fully by the parent. It is, in no uncertain terms, how Ninja began the first stage of 『Mu Sei』 Shūgyō. When all of Ninjutsu is put together, the fact that the foundation on which everyone's rests has its root in this cannot be ignored.

In addition, the 『Ninjutsu no Yoko Aruki』 , which appeared in the 『Mu Kei』 section as well as the 『Mu Seki』 section also comes on the scene here as if looking for a role. No, no, no while this Yoko Aruki fellow can be a bit of a troublesome fellow, when speaking of the abilities of held within Ninjutsu, the spectacularly fearful level it was, was not apparent head on. Instead it splayed out unhesitatingly in four directions across eight lines. It cannot be moved from the position it occupies. In the end we must consider that listening to what this crab-walk fellow boasts regarding the ins and outs of his skill would be akin to delving into the depths or Oku of Ninjutsu.

In other words, if we take a look at 『Ninjutsu no Yoko Aruki』 as to how it applies only to the section on 『Mu Sei,』 one would find that it is much like what was detailed in the section on 『Mu Kei.』 Facing sideways with the hips placed loosely above the legs, thereby causing the narrowest portion of the body to interact with the air. Progress is made by fully extending the thighs and following this by crossing and then uncrossing the legs repeatedly. A perfected crab-walk will cause the hips to act like a spring, naturally giving power to the feet to allow a gentle *Shina-shina* or elastic, progress. In other words, as the feet do not impact roughly on the ground so this flexible[1] way of walking or way of stepping coupled with the advantage of minimizing the impact with the surrounding air results in footfalls that cannot be heard. This is area where 『Mu Sei』 is most effective and where it is most spectacular. As the foundation is built up and strengthened from walking across the dampened *Tōshi* paper one can begin to nod in understanding as to why the Yoko Aruki of 『Mu Sei』 can be so effective. We find that it is this crab-walk fellow that is both present and fully adaptable within in 『Mu Kei,』 『Mu Seki』 and 『Mu Sei.』 That Ninjutsu of the past used this over such a wide range cannot come as a surprise.

---

[1] 軟らかい *Yawarakai*. Can mean both soft and flexible.

An illustration of a father and son performing *Shūgyō* in *Musei.*

◎ 解圖子親者忍と業修の聲無 ◎

This is a scene depicting the first *Shūgyō*.

With a treat already prepared as a reward, the father takes the child by the hand and walks him across the wet *Tōshi* paper.

Little by little.

無息の修行（六無の五）

Shūgyō Method for Conducting Shūgyō in Mu Soku, Breathless

(*Roku Mu Number Five*)

The one in fifth position 『*Mu Soku*』 is one level harder. This 『*Mu Soku*』 and the following remaining one 『*Mu Shū*』 are built atop the foundation Ninja created with the silent method of walking of 『*Mu Sei*』 through the Shūgyō of walking across dampened *Tōshi* paper. There is a strong link here, namely that if 『*Mu Soku*』 and 『*Mu Shū*』 are not joined in unison then 『*Mu Sei*』 alone cannot reach the fullest extent of its potential. In other words, if we take 『*Mu Sei*』 to be the principal then 『*Mu Soku*』 and 『*Mu Shū*』 become subordinate. That being said, being the "principal" does in no way diminish the others' standing rather the principal and the subordinate are interdependent and mutually supportive. This is the crucial element that dictates the effectiveness of this.

Clearly the Shūgyō in 『*Mu Soku*』 is on a level of difficultly higher than 『*Mu Sei*』 and it follows that 『*Mu Shū*』 is more difficult still. Again, within the realm of Ninjutsu recognizing the value (worth) of this is essential. In addition it allows us to step deeper into the realm occupied by Ninjutsu, and see the dignity (level) which this method for hammering and kneading the human form can achieve. Knowing then that both these methods of Shūgyō are within Ninjutsu will no doubt grant improbable insight into them.

Well then, we are on the subject of 『*Mu Soku.*』 Mu Soku can be thought of as "Without breath" or Shūgyō in eliminating breathing. Clearly one cannot simply stop breathing because you'll, you know, die so we must avoid useless banter. What this actually represents is a Ninjutsu-style description. A correct definition would be to say when breathing one moves the surrounding air, so in order to prevent people from sensing your presence, both the indrawn air and expelled air are done silently[1]. Shūgyō is done so that breathing becomes so gentle as it

---

[1] 静かに *Shizuka ni*. This word can mean both "silent" and "still."

almost seems to not be present. It must be noted that breathing is linked
to the heart. Should the heart begin to move, then breathing will
rebound from this. If the heart is disturbed then the breathing will be
correspondingly ragged, thus in order to maintain a gentle breathing first
the heart must be pacified. Regardless of the circumstances one cannot
flinch or start, and it is essential to master *Fu-dō-shin*[1]. Once the *Fu-dō-
shin* has been drilled into the body and control of the breathing one is
born with has been completed, next we can return to the beginning and
join the twin resources of controlled breathing and *Fu-dō-shin* together.
I would like to add a final point; while this is of great use within Ninjutsu,
it can be also of use to people as a method strengthening and disciplining
the body.

Thus the Shūgyō of Ninja in 『Mu Soku』 begins at an extremely
young age. They would submerge their heads in wooden barrels or metal
basins filled to the top with pure water and work to extend the time they
could hold their breath. The eyes, rather than being shut, are held open
which teaches the sense that one can look about with ease underwater.
One was taught to seek the limits one could *Gaman*[2]. This information
will prove useful when we reach the section on 『Sui Ton no Jutsu』 in
the next chapter.

Once a child comes of age and begins to understand something of
how the world works real Shūgyō in Ninjutsu begins.[3] The method
consists of taking a single strand from a silkworm cocoon and putting
glue on one end of that thin string affix one end to the edge of the nose
near the nostril[4]. Another is placed on the other side. Bringing ones face
close to a somewhat less than glamorous mirror one plays a game.
Finding a place where one can see clearly, close the mouth firmly and
breathe solely from the nose. Concentrating solely on breathing in a
manner so that wisp of silt does not so much as flutter with a *Soyo*[5]. This
can only be achieved by deep gentle breathing. So when viewed the
thread cannot be said to be either moving or not. Keep your eyes riveted
to it.

---

[1] 不動心 Immovable heart. Firmness of purpose or character.
[2] 我慢 Endure. In this case how long you can hold your breath.
[3] 物心を附く *Mono-gokoro wo tsuku*. Becoming aware of things around
you and other people. Reaching the age of discretion.
[4] 孔
[5] ソヨ Soyo as in そよ風 Soyo-Kaze-slight breeze.

Undoubtedly at first ensuring that the silk thread does not waver with a *Soyo* will be rather difficult going. As I mentioned before if the heart begins to become even a little bit disturbed, it will immediately echo in the breathing. Clearly here as well, maintaining *Fu-dō-shin* is of upmost importance. So then, heartbeat and breathing controlled without the most infinitesimal disturbance. Shūgyō is built up through silently, silently, gently, gently breathing. Gradually, the body begins to learn and after a great length of time, the movement of thread of silk, at some point, has decreased. When it has ceased to move one can be said to have graduated from this particular Shūgyō.

This requires the application of a great deal of willpower and unifying heartbeat and breath is not something, *not something* that can be done easily. The realization of this Shūgyō is something that, first and foremost is going to be of great assistance to the *Ō-rai-shin-tai*[1] of Ninja. While this power may seem to reside unobtrusively in the shadows, it is due to its effectiveness that it is so highly prized. A Ninja can walk without sound by using the Shūgyō of 『*Mu Sei*』, but should the breathing of that same Ninja cause turbulence then irrespective of the deepness of the darkness that surrounds their body, something will set off the enemy. It is said if this happens then when attempting to move in on an enemy position, their sharper than average senses will immediately detect your *Kehai*[2]. A Chinese Taoist once said:

> *Simpletons breathe through their mouths, intellectuals breathe through their noses, the common folk breath through both, experts breathe through Heso*[3] *and holy men through the heels.*

Those Ninja who have completed the 『*Mu Soku*』 Shūgyō are within the realm of the "expert" or those who 『*breathe through Heso.*』 Should they have further refined their skills then all that is left is to rise to the level of holy man and those who breathe 『*through the heels.*』 At this point Ninjutsu seems to be reaching nearly comically heavenly heights as it is able to respond to all trials and tribulations unhindered. Again here I wish to include the point that through the Ninjutsu Shūgyō of 『*Mu Soku*』 anyone can strengthen and form themselves.

---

[1] 往来進退-Comings and goings, enterings and exitings.
[2] 気配 Sense of presence.
[3] 臍 Belly button.

無臭の修業法（六無の六）[1]

Method for conducting Shūgyō in *Mu Shū*, Odorless.

(*Roku Mu* Number Six)

At last we have reached the final "Mu" that all of the 『Roku Mu』draw their power from, the one in sixth position 『*Mu Shū.*』This fellow is, well, a bit of a bastard. Even saying that, know that there is a deep underlying feeling to this, based on real life or death experiences. The extent to which Ninja devoted themselves, plumbing the depths to come up with these concepts can only, *only* astonish us today. Continuously performing this Shūgyō with its focus on self-denial seems to be a test as to how much a person can *Gaman*![2] Probably Zen monks and *Risshū*[3] monks as well wouldn't be willing to label them "a living Buddha[4]" or a "master priest," but then I don't know. Then there are the block-headed priests who fill up the mountain huts[5], who are generally of the sort who have secretly let diligence fall by the wayside. And neck and neck with those fellows as to who can fall off the path set by their religion the furthest, are the overtly *Niku-jiki-sai-tai.*[6] The Shūgyō done by Ninja is in *complete* contrast to this. Even secretly breaking a prohibition would mean the end as it would immediately result in 『*Nin no Yabure.*』 Tens of years of blood and sweat wrung out by Shūgyō can be scattered in all directions by one fault. One's gifts and one's very life would be rapidly pulled away in a single agonizing moment. Not only Ninja but also regular people can through this strengthen and harden

---

[1] In some editions of this book the character for "breathe"息 was mistaken for "smell"臭. The corrected version is here.
[2] 我慢 Enduring, sucking it up.
[3] Risshū (律宗?) school of Buddhism is one of the six schools of Nara Buddhism in Japan, The Ritsu school was founded in Japan by the blind Chinese priest Jianzhen, better known by his Japanese name "Ganjin." Ganjin traveled to Japan at the request of Japanese priests, and established the Toshodai Temple in Nara.
[4] 活佛 *Iki-botoke*. A person living an austere lifestyle.
[5] 大道店 *Daidō-ten*. Small make shift shops along a travelling path.
[6] 肉食妻帯 Referring to Buddhist monks who ate meat and had wives, which was forbidden.

themselves, in other words, a method of *Tanren*[1] for the body. 『*Mu Shū*』 must be seen then as looking down at 『*Mu Soku*』 to a degree. This is not writing about something that could possibly have an effect, *how then do you plan on making your case?* you ask.

While this method of Shūgyō does not at first glance appear to be difficult, the degree to which one must *Gaman* becomes quite, *quite* problematic. First off, even should it be anathema to you, Ninja absolutely do not consume alcohol. They absolutely do not smoke tobacco. They absolutely do not eat spicy, aromatic or oily foods. Second, despite any proclivity you may have, sweet as well as excessively salty things must be abstained from. Third, hot water, tea, and large amounts of water should not be drunk. Fruits must be eaten sparingly. This seems to indicate that most food items consumed by humans are off limits, and one is tempted to say bewildered "You are not allowed to eat anything!" No, despite the 『*Nin*』 of Ninjutsu being the same 『*Nin*』 of Nintai[2] or endurance, the answer to the question "Why is it Ninja must ban such a wide range, such a ridiculous range of foods? *Gaman* or *Nintai* must be carried to such extremes?" The reasoning behind this is wholly un-mysterious.

First thought let us see what we can derive from the following statement:

> *Thus it is said that this is for removing smells from the body.*

Humans in fact smell of humans. The stink of the body or, in other words the odor. Making a broad sketch, dogs stink of canine, cats reek of feline, horses smell of equine, cows smell of bovine, pigs are the thing that smell the most like swine and sheep are undoubtedly ovine in odor. Lions, tigers and all the beasts of prey, each, each has a particular stink about it. Anyway, you look at it the smell of an elephant is considerable, while birds each smell according to the odor associated with that variety. The "fishy" smells particular to a species of aquatic creature are certainly discernable. When it comes to varieties of insects things become a bit more complicated, though we do have the stink bug[3] which one needs to

---

[1] 鍛錬 Forging. Used in martial arts to refer to hardening both the body and spirit.

[2] 忍耐 Endure. Put up with.

[3] 屁っ放り虫 *Heppiri Mushi*. Amusingly written as the fart-releasing-bug.

watch out for. Mankind never hesitates in its confidence in mastery over the natural world, yet here one can't help but think that if all the creatures inhabiting the earth came at you at once, their sharp words would make you think the fart of a stink bug was not so bad. Those born with a naturally effusive odor from the armpits, bad breath or those whose illnesses resist treatment are clearly not in a position to apply to be a Ninja. Eliminating them from the discussion we turn to focus with a wry smile on the fact that Chinese smell like Chinese and hairy foreigners smell like hairy foreigners. Be that at it may that westerners may think that because Japs eat rice all the time that they smell like rats to a degree that can scarcely be endured, causing him to turn that nose long-as-a-dripping-candle away. Of course the people that inhabit the Asian countries of which the Japanese are a member of do not think they reek of rat. This is probably due to the fact that as they have the same smell it sort of cancels out. I am not going to go so far as to state that Japanese should stop eating rice and as this is somewhat beside the point we will leave it at that. When speaking of the smell of each and every person know that even within a single household, if individually examined the differences emanating from them would be quite surprising indeed.

So we will first delve into the multitude of possible body smells of humans and how the nose cannot help but categorize them. In the first part we have those that favor alcohol have a ripe persimmon smell about them, tobacco lovers, it goes without saying reek of nicotine resin. Those who enjoy chili powder and spicy seasonings have an odor that pricks at the inner nose. The particular odor of onions, green onions, garlic and such are sensed sharply in the nose. The smells of those that favor

alcohol, smoke tobacco, enjoy spicy and strongly seasoned^{garlicy} foods in large amounts are rapidly apparent to those who consume smaller amounts of the same. To those who are teetotalers, non-smokers, adverse to spicy foods or dislike strongly seasoned^{garlicy} foods those smells can be offensive even to the point where they become nauseated and need to escape from it. That there are people who find certain foods that unbearable must be kept in mind. Those that are downwind of one of these people emitting all manner of smell have no choice but to clearly remember them. Now, would you most kindly suppose there is a dog about downwind? Maybe it is somewhere between a Chō or half-Chō distant[1]. This little shit is

---

[1] 町 A unit of measure covering a distance of 109.9 meters.

going to have a sharp, highly refined sense of sme ll. Without a doub t it
^{n o s e o n   h i m   n o   m i s t ake}
will start barking with a *Wan! Wan!* sound. The fact of the matter is
Ninja have to consider alcohol, tobacco, spicy seasoning, and the smells
^{g a r l i c y}
of strongly seasoned foods as being a greater threat than poisons or
sedatives.

   While the sweet foods and the heavily salted foods that make up the
second part are not necessarily on another order of danger to the first,
excessive consumption of sweets will result in a body smell that will be
offensive to those not predisposed to such foods. Kind of a lukewarm,
vaguely rotten smell. Somewhat more unusual is the body of a person
^{flavored}
who has a taste for heavily salted foods. When that smell reaches the
^{flavored}
senses of that, admittedly uncommon, person who dislikes such salted
foods it's like a double punch as it seems to fill and stick to the nose. In
summary we have two extremes. It all seems quite obvious and for us we
need not concern ourselves with the above, yet for the Ninja alone it is
essential. None of the above elements can be ignored. The deadly
serious warnings that accompany training are not something that can be
cast aside. All things being equal however, this is not saying one can
never eat any of the above, rather *consuming them excessively* is warned
against. The degree to which they can be eaten is the question. Everyone
has some kind of food they are fond of and despite the fact that they are
Ninja, they are human. Should all of these things, Sake, tobacco, spicy
^{flavored}
foods, salted foods be banned, along with and especially, sweets and
seasoned foods, we have to consider then one's reason for living will be
affected. I think we can all agree that what this comes down to is the
degree to which things that will affect people who dislike sweet things or
^{spicy}
dislike salty foods can be consumed so that one's smell will not become
an issue. Considering it to be a balance between humanity and suffering
will have us nodding in agreement.

   For the next section, the third, the tenor changes just a bit. Hot
water, tea and other liquids cannot be drunk with abandon while
watermelon, musk melon, Asian pears, peaches, *Mikan*[1] and other such

---

[1] 蜜柑 *Mikan* or tangerine (a multitude of other names as well) native to
Japan. Formally known as the 温州蜜柑 Unshu Mikan named for a city
in China, where the same Kanji are used to describe it. The Japanese

Mizu-gashi or fruit-candies[1] cannot be consumed recklessly. The reason being one will have to urinate longer and more frequently, in other words in the serious pursuit of their objective this will result in a hindrance to Ninja. The cautions related to this are many and have little to do with smell but rather concern that which is outlined above. But come to think of it, no, this certainly concerns body smell. Whether speaking of musk melon, *Mikan* or that *Mikan*-like *Navel Orange*[2], as these kinds of *Mizu-gashi* are aromatic, they will serve as the base to give rise to odors. It is a known fact that those who have a weakness for *Mikan* tend to end up with a vaguely yellowish tint to their skin. If you are trying to surprise people more than this you will have to show up with your whole body reeking of orange. Further, even the so called banana,[3] while not particularly juicy gives off a rather florid aroma. I am not speaking of the firm green ones that come from Taiwan but rather the fully ripe ones from the rain forests of Singapore with their absurdly strong smell. After consuming one of these, wiping off the resulting sweat with a handkerchief will have everything smelling of its perfume. Almost as a bonus these have the ability to give one frequent urination that reeks fantastically of bananas, with an odor similar to *Albos* or *Kureshin* in

---

name is a result of the local reading of the same characters used in Chinese. In both languages, the name meaning "Honey Citrus of Wenzhou", a city in China.

[1] 水菓子 Fruit was known as "water candy" in Japanese, though now most commonly referred to as 果物 *Kuda mono* which means "fruit thing."

[2] *Citrus sinensis*. This orange varietal is the result of a single mutation which occurred on a plantation in Brazil in 1820. The mutation led to the formation of a conjoined twin enclosed within the rind of a seedless orange, and it proved to be a hit, so people began cultivating it in other regions. Because the navel orange is seedless, it can only be propagated through cuttings. Technically, every navel orange comes from the same orange tree; the Brazilian orange which generated a spontaneous mutation hundreds of years ago. Orange farmers take cuttings from their navel orange trees and graft them onto fresh stock periodically to ensure that their orchards stay healthy.

[3] 香蕉 Itoh Sensei uses the Chinese word for banana here implying that it is a bit of a newfangled thing. The Japanese originally referred to it as either 甘蕉 *Kanshō* or 実芭蕉 *Mibashō*.

intensity[1]. With respect to Ninja this one is strictly off limits.

Thus each of these factors must be dealt with. The Ninjutsu Shūgyō of eliminating the smells of the body are strict to the degree that they resemble the admonishments of a monk towering, *towering* so high that one can scarcely see their feet. The incredible devotion to killing the heart and banishing desire is something that exceeds even the most pious of priests. One has to wonder when these devotions will surpass that same priest up. Don't get the idea that I am trying to be clever here but as was stated previously, those *Kashira-bun* working directly for a noble house would feel the weight of their responsibility and take due precautions with their Shūgyō. On the other hand were we to peek in on the Ninja underlings in the lower ranks we would likely find they furtively circumvent these regulations with a *Choi-Choi* occasional disregard.

Were we to take the time to scrutinize the whole 『*Mu Shū*』 again, to ensure nothing was overlooked, we would find that though the path of an expert hunter is very different, were we to join his half with ours we would find *Pitari*[2] a perfectly matching *Warifu*[3]. The reason for this is that whether it be a deer, wild boar or a bear, the Shūgyō that leads to the path a master hunter must take to bring down any of the large game beasts is one of considerable, *considerable* difficulty. While that Shūgyō contains many elements, of primary import is limiting the smell of "human stink" from the razor sharp senses of wild beasts. There is no alternative to the "killing the heart and banishing desire" which was spoken of earlier. Temperance, abstaining from *Sake* and refraining from spicy foods or garlicky foods. In the end this *Gaman* of certain foods is identical to the methods employed in the Shūgyō of becoming a master hunter. No matter what path you are on, in order to reach the highest ranks, this level of Shūgyō is clearly essential. Be that as it may, amongst those hunters there may well be some who have a liking for tea

---

[1] These were written as アルボース and クレシン. One is a brand of disinfectant and the other possibly a cleanser. Whatever they are clearly they both smell bad and I am not going to spend all day researching them.
[2] ピッタリ The sound of something fitting together perfectly.
[3] 割符 A piece of paper, bamboo, wood or sometimes even bronze with a stamp or mark put on it which is then split in two. Used for passing checkpoints and proving who you are.

or sweets, yet the admonition 『consuming them excessively』 that holds true for Ninja is not there.

We are now at the end of the explanation of the 『Roku Mu.』 While the above can be thought of as the *I, Ro, Ha,*[1] or ABC's, of Ninjutsu that the Ninja of the past learned, to term this as something that leads directly to Ninjutsu would be an error. This is nothing more than the preferred first step. Consider then that these six varieties, these six stages of Shūgyō take the inborn operation^(movement) of the body, in other words 『Honno Sayo』 or instinctive response. Should these stages not be kneaded and worked in such a manner as to be identical to these inherent abilities, embarking on training in the larger realm of Ninjutsu is all but impossible. Due to the nature of the restrictions and regulations of long ago, Ninja had to pass through the gates of this test. To be successful it required, above all else, a supreme level of commitment and seriousness of purpose.

In the end, the *I,Ro,Ha* beginning is just that. As we will build the structure of Ninjutsu atop it, the earthen base must be formed. While this foundation is still not surely^(firmly) in place, nary a single column of can be placed with certainty. Any half-measured should be refrained from and bull-headedly attempting to erect a building will only result in a *Yota-yota* unsteady, *Gura-gura* irregular, painful to witness sort of Ninjutsu. Something that won't stand up in wind or earthquake. Using it once will only invite 『*Nin no Yabure*』 as everything falls helplessly apart and in the end one's life becomes forfeit. Returning to the example of the foundation we used before and extending it one step, 『*Mu Sei,*』 which holds the beginnings of the 『Roku Mu,』 serves to form the initial layer of this base with 『Walking across dampened Toshi.』 Leaping upward from the Shūgyō of 『*Mu Sei*』 we have 『*Mu Soku*』 and 『*Mu Shū*』 which brace it from either side. Unquestioningly the first step will be to undertake the creating of your foundation through 『*Roku Mu.*』 This having been completed and your Shūgyō in 『*Roku Mu*』 each and every of those fundamental, core elements of the 『*Roku Mu*』 will serve as the starting point for launching into the establishment of a foundation in the whole of Ninjutsu. There will be no shaking like a drunken indigent as

---

[1] イ ロ ハ The old progression of the Japanese Hiragana alphabet. Now it is アイウ A,I,U.

you successfully complete the elements of your mission.

Looking back at what we have gone over hopefully the explanation of 『Roku Mu』 has been laid out clearly as the author has gone to great lengths to ensure this. All of this has been done with the idea of laying the groundwork for dealing with the question of how Ninjutsu can be applied in these modern times. Examining what the Ninjutsu of the past was like, thus the first thing we must look at is uncovering the method of firming up the foundation with 『Roku Mu.』 With this point as a start, the rest should fall into line. Therefore we now move to take a step beyond the foundation built through 『Roku Mu』 and examine that which rests at the next level. At this juncture I will stop my brush and I encourage you to look over what has been said. If not I am libel to just go on and on.

其の二、古への忍者の練習法は餘りに酷烈過ぎた (中)

Chapter Two: The training undergone by Ninja of the past was unbelievably severe. (Middle Section)

So then, in rather short order we have wrapped up the 『Roku Mu.』 Having firmly packed down our foundation, at long last the time has come to switch gears and set about the construction of our building. I suppose then we must raise the main pillar of Ninjutsu first...No, before that we have a little bit of work to do. Looking at the foundation of a house that has been built, you will find that the money safe has been placed on a raised stone step. Or, sometimes an object of importance or a revered ^precious thing will be set on a stone dais. Whatever it may be, surrounding this, a firm wooden framework is set up with the floor laid on top of that. At the same time, this also serves to act as a guard against robbery...clearly one cannot take the construction of a building's foundation lightly. It goes without saying of course that the foremost consideration when assembling the eccentric, unconventional building that is Ninjutsu, with its indescribably singular order, *is the foundation*. Thinking that the 『Roku Mu』 is the entirety of this foundation would be an error. No. Clearly there are other things and they should all be erected on the spot in a structure where nothing except the cash safe, item of extreme value or revered ^precious object would be place should be used. We are after all attempting to assemble a whole new kind of mechanism.

Here we must take the results of the Shūgyō in 『Roku Mu』 and join it with *Honkaku*[1] Ninjutsu Shūgyō. Our mid-term goal being the taking on of what is known as the 『Shi-U no Shūgyō』 . We are, in other words, ^picking out plucking out four protrusions sticking up from our foundation. When compared to the 『Roku Mu』 which should be ingrained while still in childhood, this is primarily a training to be undertaken upon reaching adulthood. So then, having worked diligently to acquire the skills of the 『Roku Mu』 now, at last, we may begin to draw a bit of profit from it. I humbly request your upmost attention for

---

[1] 本格 Implies both "serious" and "full-on" as well as "genuine" or "serious."

this thing known as the 『Shi-U no Shūgyō.』 Observe, if you will, how the 『Shi-U』 stands in contrast to the 『Roku Mu.』 While the 『Roku Mu』 consists of Shūgyō in ^{causing} crafting nothingness out of something that exists, the 『Shi-U』 is Shūgyō in taking something that exists and having it remain as such. While this would seem to indicate a complete dichotomy, in the end, well....they ^{operate} work in unison, revealing, I think, the unique flavor of Ninjutsu that is embedded therein.

But, my dear friends I humbly request that you do not give into surprise upon hearing the term 『Shi-U.[1]. And they are the following four:

Thus we have 『凡胎を脱するの術 Bontai wo Da suru no Jutsu』 or The Art of Separating Oneself from the Mortal Flesh.

Thus we have 『飛行自在の術 Hikō Jizai no Jutsu』 or The Art of Self-preservation Through Flying.

Thus we have 『昇天の術 Shoten no Jutsu』 or The Art of Ascension.

Thus we have 『縮地の術 Shukuchi no Jutsu』 or The Art of Shrinking Distance.

To be frank I understand that simply hearing such names

---

[1] 四有 Rather clumsily translates to "The Four Is" (The character 有 means "is" or "exists" and is the opposite of 無 Mu or "nothingness". "Is(ness)" isn't really a word and "The Four Are" seems rather unwieldy to boot. This term would perhaps be surprising to Japanese readers at the time because within Buddhism, practiced extensively within Japan, there is already a well-known 『Shi-U』 "The Four Existences" reflecting the four stages on the cycle/wheel of life:
I.	The very second life begins is 生有 Shi-U or birth.
II.	The time from birth to death is 本有 Hon-U or life.
III.	The moment life ends is 死有 Shi-U or death.
IV.	The period where one awaits rebirth is 中有 Chu-U or limbo.
Now Itoh Sensei is introducing the 『Shi-U』 for Ninjutsu.

causes one to imagine that they are all mystic unknowable magical techniques, but consider the fact that we referred to the 「Roku Mu」 as being "Shūgyō" and not "techniques" as such. Without a doubt there is a "Shūgyō" element to the 「Shi-U」 but we also have the label "technique" carved firmly into it. What this all comes down to is when putting the 「Roku Mu」 in Honkaku Ninjutsu Shūgyō it becomes clear that the 「Shi-U」 are a step further along. We have no choice other than to cock our heads at this somewhat puzzling aspect the Ninjutsu of the past placed so much emphasis on. Let us now proceed onto a breakdown of each of the 「Shi-U.」

凡胎を脱するの術（四有の一）

The Art of Separating Oneself From the Mortal Flesh

(The First of the Shi-U)

The first one in line is 『*Bontai wo Da suru no Jutsu*』. This Separating Oneself from the Mortal Flesh means, in fact, taking the body of a living thing born from a human body and lifting its spirit to a level beyond that of flesh and blood. The reasoning is that through this one can achieve a *Ji-yu-ji-zai*[1] level of movement beyond that which is sought by ordinary man. Note that these are the words of Sennin of China and therefore the names of the techniques are naught but tomfoolery and can hardly be said to be part of the vernacular. The reality is not nearly so mysterious. To break this down, well, simply it is nothing more than a variety of physical exercise designed to lighten the body. In other words, unlike the Shūgyō of the 『Roku Mu』 this waza is something that can be done out in the open. Here again we can peek in again on the mischievous life style that the Sennin showed a liking for. Taking this into consideration their outlandish ways and foolishness can be seen as amusing. We do however have the line 『重裘を被りて山谷を馳駆す。 *Jyūkyū wo Kaburite Sankoku wo Chiku su* or "Donning the *Jyūkyū* and charging over and through mountains and valleys."』 To lay out the entirety of this Shūgyō would be too long and undoubtedly leave everyone going *Oh my, Oh my,* as their spirits are confounded. Should one earnestly undertake this Shūgyō in the field, however one will no longer consider it to be a simple "waza."

As for the explanation for how this is done, it is as inscribed below: The *Jyūkyū* is a heavy cowl of skin[2]. It is a kind of winter clothing fashioned from the hides of beasts sewn together. First of all, let us

---

[1] 自由自在 Complete freedom of movement. Completely in control.

[2] 重裘 The character 裘 can be read as *Kawagoromo* which means "hood of skin." An ancient Chinese winter coat made from various animal hides, particularly fox and a kind of small black sheep called a *Kou* 羔. The first kanji 重 refers to a doubling or a particularly heavy *Kawagoromo*.

imagine that it is already hot, and then we introduce the *Jyūkyū*, resulting in an almost painful level of heat. That heavy, oppressive heat—outfitted not unlike John crying in the open field[1]. And, in that guise, go just as is written in the phrase 『...charging over and through mountains and valleys.』 Well, well, well, this is hardly something one can term a silly game. When we speak of "mountains and valleys" this is quite different from the relative flats of Sanya town[2] within Tokyo proper.

---

[1] This is a translation of Itoh Sensi's quote. John the Baptist (sometimes called John in the Wilderness) A saint who's calling was to prepare the way for the coming of the Messiah. He lived in the wilderness of Judea between Jerusalem and the Dead Sea. The description of his apparel is:

> *His raiment of camel's hair, and a leather girdle about his loins; and his meat was locusts and wild honey.*

The most likely quote I could find regarding Itoh Sensei's reference was when John says, quoting the prophet Isaiah:

> *'I am the voice of one calling in the desert, Make straight the way for the Lord,'*. John 1:23

John the Baptist described himself as "the voice ... crying out in the wilderness."

[2] Sanya (山谷) the Kanji for which are "mountain-valley" is an area in the Taitō district of Tokyo though it has been broken up and renamed. The area was the residence of a pre-Meiji era Burakumin 部落民. Burakumin were modern-day descendants of Japan's feudal outcast group. They were originally members of outcast communities in the Japanese feudal era, composed of those with occupations considered impure or tainted by death (such as executioners, undertakers, workers in slaughterhouses, butchers or tanners), which have severe social stigmas of *kegare* (穢れ or "defilement") and were referred to as Eta 穢多, literally, "an abundance of defilement." Though officially abolished long ago parts of Japan discrimination against this group and its accompanying low socio-economic status persists. "Sanya" along with other Burakumin communities weren't shown on maps because traditionally the Burakumin weren't considered fully human nor were their members counted in censes. This area also contains Namidabashi 泪橋 where prisoners said their final goodbye's to loved ones at a canal before they were taken to the adjacent Kozukappara execution grounds 小塚原刑場 *Kozukappara keijō* (an estimated 100,000-200,000 executions took

This refers to the ideal location for the domicile of a Sennin, namely deep mountains plunging into valleys, interlaced with roads that may or may not in fact actually be roads. A decidedly dangerous place, therefore being encumbered by that *Jyūkyū* we've been going on about as one shoots over a precipice, scrambles up boulders or dashes about would be an arduous affair indeed. A drum beat pounding out a dance rhythm like to tear the leather drum head is naught but the beating heart. The body tires. Our breath is heaving. Flames seem to leap from our mouth. Eyes are shot with blood. On top of all this sweat pours off us due to the heat. The steam billowing from the top of our *Jyūkyū* is such that we could easily make use of it for 『霧隠れの術 *Kiri-gakure no Jutsu* The Art of Escaping With Fog.』 This is a hard way, a brutal way, a violent way, a way bordering on the absurd. One would be shocked to hear someone describe this as "a playful diversion." Speaking frankly this is hardly ᵘⁿˡⁱᵏᵉˡʸ seems something that can be endured.

We cannot laugh this off as a thankless task like to leave one with half the bones in their body splintered. It is, in the end, a way to test oneself. Diligently, seriously, unbendingly, tirelessly, without losing heart, without becoming sloppy. Bravely, intensely, and if the worst case occurs, being prepared for the ultimate sacrifice in a calm manner. This training done in a full-on all out blaze of action is fearfully effective. Excessive fat will be cleanly wrung from the body by the *Jyūkyū* as if we had placed ourselves on a *Shime-gi*[1]. Sweaty oils will flow off in a thick *Doro Doro* and a sticky *Neba-neba* sound. The body will be thin and lean while the muscles have shrunk hard against the frame. Knocking ones hand against it will result in an audible reply as if it were iron.

The three-hundred-sixty joints of the body that act as springs are all

---

place here) , now covered with railway tracks. Presently it is a region with a distinct culture, an area of crowded, cheap rooming houses where day laborers live, though in recent years, some of the rooming houses have converted to provide cheap accommodation for foreign backpackers. So Itoh Sensei's reference has a lot of connotations.

[1] 締め木 or 搾め木 A wooden device consisting of two boards between which nuts or vegetables are placed and heavy pressure is applied in order to extract oil. Also used to refer to someone (wringing) working the body into shape.

strengthened[1]. Each and every of the eighty-four thousand pores of the body become mouths to respire spiritual energy[2]. A form with a lightness that has been completely (utterly) altered from how it came into this world. A vigorousness is present as is a resonant spirit and thus the physical form is taken off like a cicada emerging from its nymph skin. The feeling is of

---

[1] While this "360" number has been calculated as:

 Skull= 86 Throat= 6 Thorax= 66 Spine / Pelvis= 76 Arms= 64 Legs= 62

The number of joints varies between children and adults and even between other adults. Defining a "joint" is also problematic. The skull is made up of a number of bony plates that most consider a single unit as they don't move. The figure 360 appears in the Quran and by the Chinese Confusionist Dong Zhongshu (195?–105? BCE), who in the *Chunqiu fanlu* 春秋繁露 or *Luxuriant Gems of the Spring and Autumn Annals,* in the section entitled "How human Beings Second the Numbers of Heaven," he states:
   "Human beings have 360 joints because this exactly matches the number of Heaven's [days]. Their bodies, their bones and flesh, match the thickness of the earth. Their ears and eyes are bright and keen like the qualities of the sun and moon, and in their bodies there are hollows and veins like the configurations of the rivers and valleys."
Dialogues on Eastern Wisdom. p47. Ji Xianlin et al.

[2] Here is another half-page footnote:

The Buddhists say there are 84,000 pores in a man's body and thus, by following corruption and passing through transmigration, he leaves behind him 84,000 particles of miserable dust. Buddha's body has 84,000 pores, but by resisting evil and reverting to truth he has perfected 84,000 relics; these are as hard and bright as diamonds, affording benefit to men...wherein they are deposited."
A residence among the Chinese inland, on the coast, and at sea. Being a narrative of scenes and adventures during a third visit to China, from 1853 to 1856. By Robert Fortune. Published 1857. p35. (They were all about some long titles in 1857)
And FYI:
   You must concentrate day and night, questioning yourself through every one of your 360 bones and 84,000 pores.

From *The Gateless Gate* 無門關. A collection of 48 Zen 公案 *Koans* or dialogues designed to provoke "great doubt" compiled in the early 13th century by the Chinese Zen master Wumen Hui-k'ai 無門慧開(1183–1260).

having cast something off somewhere. Should one correctly and unmistakably carry out 『Bontai wo Da suru no Jutsu』 then your *self* will be enlightened. The proof will be as if laid at your feet and the knowledge that your *self* can withstand and endure will become apparent.

Taking all that, were we now to consider then that one method of exercise were equivalent to any other method of exercise, then a person that has done the above will always break free of "Bon[1]." Whether it be the broad jump, whether it be the high jump, whether it be the steeplechase[2] or whether it be any other gymnastic or foot speed related competition. That they would surpass the title of "World Class Athletes" and enter the rarified air of "World Record Holders" cannot be doubted. Looking beyond this, in order to rise up, up to the level one can separate from the human form and aim at becoming a Sennin. To this end Desire, Profit, Will, Temper and Honor are abandoned along with everything else. Relying solely on a single *self* that is unencumbered by the world around it. This result is borne from one having battled through a Shūgyō that prepares them, without exaggeration, devoid of to sacrifice their very lives. This is the thing that differentiates it from sports.

With this in hand, we can see how the shift from *Sen-jutsu* Shūgyō[3] over to the realm of Ninjutsu Shūgyō involves a new seriousness, a new violent edge that reflects the human element introduced. As real as a trickle of blood. Be that as it may, note that of the 『Shi-U』, 『Bontai wo Da suru no Jutsu』 is but the first. Looking ahead it is pushing the remaining 『San-U or "Three-is"』 while looking back it draws up the entirety of the 『Roku Mu.』 There is a profound interdependency effect between these two aspects. In other words the result of a Ninja having completed this Shūgyō is akin to a cicada shedding its larval skin. The renewed flesh is changed. Looking back on what was achieved by the Shūgyō in 『Roku Mu』 and the great lengths we went to complete it, we find a whole new level of strength. And now, as we move on, the other 『San-U』 will add an even stricter lash to the equation and we will seek to harness that inertia.

---

[1] Referring to the *Bon* 凡 of *Bontai* 凡胎, or the "norm."
[2] The men's steeplechase started in the Olympics in 1900.
[3] 仙術 A word indicating techniques or the arts of the Sennin.

飛行自在の術 (四有の二)

The Art of Self-Preservation Through Flying.

(The Second of the Shi-U)

The one waiting for us in second position is 『*Hiko Jizai no Jutsu* The Art of Self-preservation Through Flying』, which has far and away a greater potential to startle peoples senses than the previous one. At a glance one is like to think, with no small amount of suspicion "What on earth is this?" The answer is that here as well the name was selected by the Sennin with the same playful trickery as always. This is probably due to the picture books and movies of today, but the reality is that regardless of the strength of the Sennin or the level of the Ninja the flesh and blood form of man cannot fly about in the sky at will. That being said, however, this is not some sort of thing to be used simply to amaze children and fools. Rather it is a spectacular Waza that through Kufū and Shūgyō evolved into its present form. When enacted the results of this Waza are spectacular and, moreover, an utterly practical technique. As this Shūgyō is also part of the 『U』 it is hardly something that can be done out of the view of people. The Ninja of the past therefore retained the designation granted by the Sennin and, in much the same way as 『*Bontai wo Da suru no Jutsu*』 the purpose of this is to conceal the true meaning from the average person. Therefore, I think, it is covered by this playful-word trickery of the Sennin as a way to ridicule or otherwise strike fear into the common folk.

At this point, at long last, let us investigate the method by which we can become proficient in 『*Hiko Jizai no Jutsu.*』 This of course requires that the Shūgyō in 『*Bontai wo Da suru no Jutsu*』 has been completed. First of all we must travel deep within the heart of the mountains to a sheer cliff some tens of *Jō*[1] in height straddling a rushing river in the valley far below. Snow is blowing, rocks tumble. Innumerable thunderbolts shake the very walls of the cliff. This is the kind of place one must select. Lay your eyes on a large chestnut tree or a *Keyaki*[2] tree

---

[1] 丈 One *Jō* is equivalent to 3.03 meters or ten *Shaku* 尺.
[2] 欅 Japanese *Zelkova* tree, a kind of Elm tree.

rooted to the edge of said precipice. Then, the first thing is to jump[1] ^{f l y} straight up off the ground and perform *Keiko* in grasping a branch a good distance from the ground. One should consider a distance of about one Jō from the top of the head a good place to start. Once this distance has been sufficiently mastered, take a small axe or other such item you happen to have on you and cut that branch down. Now, in order to achieve the goal of leaping up to the next highest branch, all the obstacles in your path should be cut away. In this manner we can gradually raise the pitch[2] of the activity until we are at the height equivalent to a pole vaulter[3]. In other words we are able to jump and grasp branches in the range of one *Jō* plus five *Shaku* to nearly two *Jō* overhead[4]. Performing at this level will allow one to attain this first Waza.

What we have to work on now is not simply leaping straight up off the ground and flying up to any old branch and seize it. Rather, it should be one that is hanging out in the thin air and drooping down over the edge of the cliff positioned as if it is trying to peer into the valley below. Select one of these branches that appear to be the least perilous and *make as if flying off the edge of the precipice*. This is the Keiko you must conduct. It is, to be sure, a no-holds-barred Waza. The eyes become dizzy looking at the rapids on the valley floor tens of *Jō* below. We are flying out over the line drawn by the cliff into nothingness. The mouth can hardly make words to describe this astounding feat. However if we were to inquire of our own body it would respond with a self-assured nod and a *Daijyobu*[5]. Further we ourselves would be completely unperturbed. No, not unperturbed, just not in fear.

---

[1] 飛 Itoh Sensei uses this Kanji, which while read *Tobu* is usually reserved for another homonym *Tobu* which is to fly. In this case it can be "Fly up the tree" or "Jump up the tree." Flying up the tree could imply running up the side of the tree much like the monk does later on rather than jumping straight up. This would be the initial step with true *Hikojizai no Jutsu* being the final stages described at the end of this chapter.

[2] ピッチ Itoh Sensei uses the English word here written in Katakana.

[3] An Olympic event since 1896.

[4] Though I know everyone is dying to calculate this for themselves, the answer is roughly 4.5~6 meters.

[5] 大丈夫 "I'm ok." "Everything is fine."

This having been thoroughly gone over *Shubi yoku*[1], we next have to contend with the next branch up. And the one after that. Moving up step by step until eventually our head pops out into the blue sky. At last we must scrutinize the fattest branch, moreover, the one that leans the furthest out over the valley. At last we can begin the third stage of our grand adventure. What happens is we hang from the branch and move hand-over-hand, *hand-over-hand*, down its length, gradually, *gradually* to the end of the branch. This limb we are speaking of, already naturally looks deep into the valley so the addition of body weight to it increases the bend. That same body now begins to sway and dangle with a *Buran-buran* sound in the empty air. A person who happened along could be forgiven for shivering while thinking of one's own hips being pulled into the valley below.

Ah, ah, quite a scene has unfolded before us. Moving to the extreme end of that branch—clearly we are at a point where we needn't be concerned the branch is likely to snap with a *Bo-kiri* sound. Next we begin to move the body, not unlike the pendulum of a grandfather clock[2], in a rocking motion. It follows then, that as the movement catches a rhythm, the span of the bounce becomes larger. The distance between the sheer precipice on this side and the lip of the opposite cliff that stands on the other side is no doubt some twenty *Ken*[3]. Looking down on it, the opposite side draws steadily nearer as we droop down and pulls steadily away as we rebound. This energy is harnessed and its strength is joined to our body, the branch is released with good timing and *Ah!* we are flying. Like a firmly struck ball we soar over the valley with a whistling *Phyu-* sound. "I am tracing a parabola" one begins to think as the action is completed *Shubi Yoku* and you drop onto the opposite rocky cliff. Without any undue hardship the person rises lightly with perhaps just the slightest stagger. This is, in other words, the success crafted from the Shūgyō based on the playful foolishness of the Sennin. It is 『*Hiko Jizai no Jutsu.*』 Should your life be something you are willing to sell off to the junk man along with other chipped antiques, I would encourage the able-bodied athletes of today to give it a go. If you feel that you are capable that is.

---

[1] 首尾良く "Done well from neck to tail."
[2] 柱時計 *Hashira Dokei*. A "Column clock" in Japanese.
[3] 間 One *Ken* is 6 *Shaku* 尺 or 1.818 m. Ten Ken is 18+ meters.

So we have the reckless ways of these Sennin, these playful tricksters with their strange pretentions and mocking ways that existed long ago in China. Regardless of how dangerous it was to carry out Ninjutsu long ago, this level of hardship, this taking of giant death-defying leaps and performing gymnastic arts while making no effort to disguise the soaring body—one is like to wonder if "Is it all necessary?" The fact of the matter is, we must understand that the Ninja of the past considered this to be an essential requirement. The reason being, one may be forced to leap from a castle wall over a moat, or, along the same lines, an extreme situation where one must rely on the branches of a pine tree whose libs are reflected in the mirror like moat. Leaping for them from a stone wall is utilizing the essence of 『Hiko Jizai no Jutsu.』

Illustration of a Ninja carrying out *Jiko-Jizai no Jutsu*.

昇天の術（四有の三）

Shoten no Jutsu or The Art of Ascension

(The Third of the Shi-U)

No doubt upon hearing about 『*Hiko Jizai no Jutsu*』 your eyes went wide and now, though we have a firm understanding, it is no place, *no place* to become careless. Well then, the next 『*Shoten no Jutsu*』 is taking the stage. A technique for climbing to the heavens. Unlike in today's world where we can rely on conveniences such as airplanes and airships, people in the past relied on techniques using their own flesh and blood bodies to reach the heavens.^ceiling This extraordinary technique must mean that we are going to start seeing people first grow the fine hair of a caterpillar and then onto a butterfly? You shouldn't laugh.

That being said, here too the crime of making a big fuss over name is occurring. Let us grind away the wily trickery of the Sennin and take out just what lies within. Should it not be enough to allow us to rise to the heavens then rest assured you will not be made to look a fool. It is a Waza that will allow you to rise, without the use of your hands, to very great heights indeed. Adding layer upon layer of Shūgyō will not, however allow any and every one to achieve it. To put it one way, as with sports take say the run up to the long jump as an example. A rhythm is found and that power is used, whether it be the stone side of a castle, a wall, a fence, or in extreme cases a cliff. In situations where it is required that hands are left free we can scurry up an obstacle with a *Datsu-datsu-datsu-datsu* scampering sound[1].

"My gosh, my golly, THIS is what Climbing to the Heavens is all about!"

"But, there is no way that could actually be done?"

No, it can be done. I will give you an example of it being done.

When this old man was but a youth and the Meiji Era[2] was still

---

[1] I believe this method where the hands are free vs using the hands is the main difference between 『*Shoten no Jutsu*』 and 『*Hikojizai no Jutsu*』.

[2] 明治時代 The "Meiji" Emperor attained the throne at the age of 14 and

relatively in its early years, I paid a visit to a country temple near my hometown. An itinerant priest happened to be visiting there from some place and he showed me a feat of near superhuman strength which astounded me. He demonstrated how he could scale, without the use of his hands the great thick, tall *Maru-bashira*[1] in the center of the main hall of that temple.

"What's this? I'll be dammed if a person can do that!

That guy is no doubt he gathers people around to get some of the offering they are carrying."

No doubt everyone's brows are furrowed with a fair amount of suspicion,

however surely there were some _{curious} gullible people about."

    The itinerant monk was in possession of a wiry and strong frame. At about forty[2] his most distinguishing feature was the intensity in his eyes. First he moved to a spot five or six *Ken*[3] back from the *Maru-bashira*, taking a pose not unlike a cat readying to go after a mouse. No, more than the pose, his countenance took on the aspect of one who has completely and somewhat disconcertingly shifted into a cat. After an interval where he glared at the *Maru-bashira* in question as if it were a mortal enemy, he let out an iron shattering Ki-ai of 『*Eih!*』 With legs whipping so fast that they could hardly be seen, he ran as if strong springs were propelling each bound as he sprinted out. In no time he had crashed into the *Maru-bashira*. My body chilled in that next

---

reigned from 1867-1912 and Itoh Sensei lived from 1871−1944. So if by "youth" we say someone of 15 years then we are looking at around 1886.

[1] 丸柱 Main column.

[2] Again with a great deal of supposition, this puts him at being born at the end of the Edo Era in the mid-1840s, before the Samurai class was abolished (The Sword Abolishment Edict issued in 1876) and all the various "countries" of Japan ruled by the *Daimyō* converted to Prefectures under the rule of the central government.

[3] 9 or 10 meters.

moment as I felt his head would split open like a melon with a *Bishari*! sound from the impact, but at that moment "What a miraculous thing! What a mysterious thing!" That great column, standing like an extension
^{fearful}
of the axis of the earth, one that neither earthquake nor great winds could affect, suddenly appears as if it leans on a diagonal like half of the letter V. The bottom of the itinerant monk's feet meet the edge of the column at the sharpened point of this character and with a *Ta' ta' ta' ta' ta' ta' ta'* and the same spring loaded quick stride, his feet grew as if hazy from the speed with which they climbed. Before one's breath could be recovered the bewildering climb was done, and, in a quick flick, a flawless backward somersault was executed before nimbly dropping back to the ground. The reality of this scene is that the column did not, in fact, lean and it was only the itinerant monk's body that leaned to "open" the V shape. It follows then that the axis of the V shape was again the monk who tilted his body and used the blinding speed that an observer would think that they had hallucinated. A slightly different way of thinking of this is to imagine getting off the train and going up and down *Kudan no Saka*[1]. The buildings on the opposite side will no doubt seem to be leaning steeply, would they not?

The itinerant monk disappeared as abruptly as he came onto the scene. Afterwards the feeling was as if an illusion had suddenly dissipated without a trace. That illusion however is still sixty-odd years later burned deep into the pupils of the author. Later, lending my ear to rumor I found out the itinerant monk was a Ninjutsu Sha from the Bakufu Era[2] and that now he was working for the government of Satsu-cho.[3] He was undoubtedly searching the whole of Japan for information.

---

[1] This fairly steep street is referred to as *Kudan no Saka* or *Kudan-zaka* is near the Nippon Budokan and Yasukuni Temple just past the Jimbocho old book shop area. The closest station is Kudanshita.

[2] Also variously referrd to as the Tokugawa bakufu 徳川幕府 and the Edo Bakufu 江戸幕府, it was the feudal Japanese military government that ruled from after the battle of Sekigahara in 1600 until the Meiji Restoration in 1867. The heads of government were all Shoguns of the Tokugawa clan.

[3] The Satsuma domain or 薩摩藩, Satsuma-han was one of the most powerful feudal domains in Tokugawa Japan, and played a major role in the Meiji Restoration and in the government of the Meiji period which followed. Most of what is today's Kagoshima prefecture, and parts of

A veritable walking covert detective. Unfortunately I was neither able to ascertain whether that rumor was true or false nor could I locate the source of it. The end result of all this is that the author had a taste of how interesting Ninjutsu was. That, in turn, was the impetus for me to investigate it further. That experience was no doubt the seed that started it all.

Ninja of the past climbed up the stone sides of castles, climbed fences and climbed walls. Other times it was used when climbing up a sheer cliff. This 『Shoten no Jutsu,』 was the thing used by that itinerant monk. The bones and flesh worked into hardened springs by 『Bontai wo Da suru no Jutsu』 serve as a qualification for this. To succeed in this requires the upmost commitment and a constant sense one's life is on the line. Being completely resolved in our actions is of the essence. This technique as well as the two previous were not something that any Ninja could do, rather undoubtedly only those at the very highest level were capable of such. In other words, this is one method of physical exercise. It should be perhaps termed the most severe, intense exercise in the world. I think we can all agree that other than those who are already Ninja, your average person is not like to be able to handle even the smallest portion of this. Again, leaping over moats, flying across valleys that clearly require the use of 『Shoten no Jutsu』 is not something within the set of tools of the average person. While we have spoken extensively on 『Shoten no Jutsu』 saying that it must be used in every situation would be a statement in need of a more discerning approach. For example, when scaling the stone wall of a castle or a cliff in many cases this technique must no doubt be utilized, but with a fence or a wall there may be situations where applying it would be bad. The reason for this being, in reality the areas the Ninja are carrying out their missions are near where people reside. Conducting 『Shoten no Jutsu』 in such a place is sure to draw the eyes and ears of people and there is a real danger of 『Nin no Yabure.』

Miyazaki prefecture in the southern island Kyushu were under its control in addition to parts of the Ryukyu or Okinawan islands which it annexed in the 16th century. The Meiji government was largely dominated by politicians from Satsuma and indeed figures from these two areas dominated the Japanese government roughly until World War I. Wikipedia.

The itinerant monk carrying out Shoten no Jutsu.

Clearly for situations where escaping in a rush is the only option, the resource that is 『*Shoten no Jutsu*』 is ideally suited in all ways. Here I am describing a method completely opposite from, and indeed rather tame in comparison to 『*Shoten no Jutsu.*』 As if from the side let us peer in at the amazing *Kufū* that are carved deep into Ninja and the way they possess neither beginning nor end. So let us get to know the methods by which the particular strategy of *Shutsubotsu-Henka*[1] is decided upon. In this case we have a wall some 8 Shaku in height that needs to be scaled.

We absolutely do not want to draw any eyes or make any sound in this situation. Here let us scrutinize the particular Katana worn on the hip of the Ninja. Understand that it is slightly shorter than normal. The blade being about 1 *Shaku* 8 *Sun* in length, with the *Saya* being about the same[2]. There is one aspect of the Saya that is particular, and that is with regards to the *Kojiri*[3]. While unobtrusive its workmanship is of a considerably more durable iron cap. The *Kojiri* is more or less slightly rounded shape with the end gradually tapering to a point.

The reason for this being that when climbing a wall it is necessary that the Ninja take the sword from off his waist. Leaving blade in the *Saya* the *Kojiri* is stuck firmly in the ground and, in this fashion when the sword is leaned against the wall it will not move. Next comes the *Sageo* which, while half as thick as a normal one, extends to nearly 7 Shaku in length. Unwrapping it from the Saya, one end is threaded through and tied in a knot while the other end is put in the mouth and held with the teeth. From there on the base of the Tsuba, which is now facing up and has been roughened with a rasp, we place the toes of one foot. Weight is gradually applied and the Ninja's body is, at the very least,

---

[1] 出没変化 Appearing and disappearing + changes.
[2] 寸 3.03 cm.
[3]

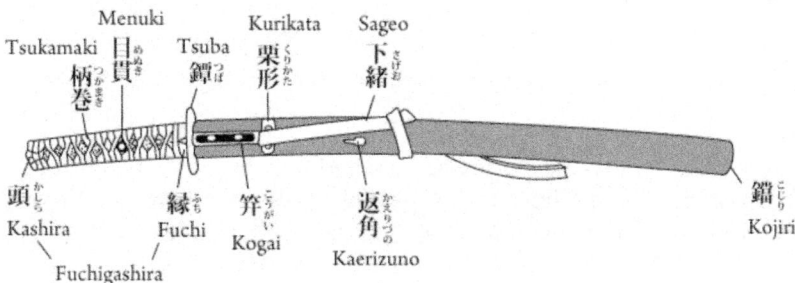

Tsukamaki	Menuki	Tsuba	Kurikata	Sageo		Kojiri

Kashira / Fuchi / Fuchigashira / Kogai / Kaerizuno

打刀拵 (うちがたなこしらえ)

2 Shaku off the ground. At this point being able to reach up and grasp the top edge of the wall would not be unimaginable. Once the fingers have the top edge of the wall it is done.

The light, conditioned body of the Ninja gets up the wall with the smooth *Suru-suru* sound of a salamander. The whole process of getting up to a prone position straddling the wall is done without any undue strain. There is a reason for lying in that prone position: while atop a wall, casually raising the upper body could, even in the midst of darkness, be spotted. Something towering atop a wall will immediately catch the enemy's eye.

You have a hindrance, by the way. As you were going up the wall, you have to deal with the issue of that thing that is usually on your hip, but was left behind when you stepped off it. Actually, as it turns out it is not a problem. The subject of the *Sageo* was brought up just for this purpose. Quickly then we reel in the *Sageo*, winding up the rope effortlessly the Katana comes up wriggling like an eel. It is then again returned to the waist and at last we drop down nimbly inside the walled area.

No, no, no. We must first pause a moment. Whether the darkness within hide some preparations crafted by the enemy or not must be determined. Should *Rankui* wooden stakes or jumbled *Sakamaki* stakes be buried in the ground, leaping down would mean getting impaled[1]. If not that then the sound given off by a falling human body, itself what can be described as a medium to large sized animal, whipping through the air with a Gou- sound would startle the sleepy nighttime atmosphere. And, no matter how light the frame may be, the vibrations given off by the impact of a body is certainly like to arouse the suspicions of the enemy.

---

[1] 亂杭 *Rankui* "wild stakes". Are stakes randomly buried in the ground at different heights sometimes with rope strung between them in order to slow/injure the attacking forces. 逆茂木 "reversed jumbled trees" *Sakamogi* can refer to either a barrier of sharpened stakes or a pit filled with a jumble of thick branches that would hinder the attackers.

忍者塀越しの心得

Demonstration of a Ninja scaling a wall.

So then, we quietly observe the scene for a time until we can nod to ourselves there is no immediate threat. After that, we hook our left hand firmly on top of the wall and put our weight on it. We gradually slide our body, now parallel across the top of the wall, to the inside and slowly lower our lower half with a *Soro-soro* sound to a hanging position. Here the soles of our feet are aligned with, and closer to, the ground. We again take time to scan the area with our upper body still in a prone position. When at last it is determined that there is no immediate danger, the hand holding our body in place is released and we drop down with a soft *Yanwari* sound. It goes without saying that should you sense something is amiss, that same one-armed grasp would be used to pull the body up. We would curl ourselves up and roll back onto the wall and return to the outside of the wall. Before one is caught in a net, retire. Though 『*Shoten no Jutsu*』 would allow a vastly quicker resolution, in this situation is not called for.

Well, as I have already discussed, one aspect of the Katana, I think outlining how that same Katana could be used to cut people would not be in vain.

The nature of the of the duty that the Ninja carry out is, as was previously described in 『忍術の七段巡環 *Ninjutsu no Nanadan Jūnkan*』 or The Seven Steps in the Cycle of Ninjutsu[1].

---

[1] This is the first time Itoh Sensei has used this specific term, though he is referring to the list in Chapter Four reprinted below:

① 引受 *Hiki-uke*. Undertaking. (Receiving and undertaking an order from a *Taishō* or superior from your own side)
② 發足 *Hossoku*. Setting out. (Setting out from your own side)
③ 道行 *Michi-yuki*. Along the trail. (Time spent in transit to your destination)
④ 到着 *Tōchaku*. Arrival. (The state of having arrived at your destination)
⑤ 仕遂 *Shitoge*. Successfully completed. (The state of having completed the task)
⑥ 道行 *Michi-yuki*. Along the trail. (Time spent in transit on your return)
⑦ 引渡 Hiki-Watashi. Handing over. (The handing over of an item collected from your destination to your *Taishō* , or superior.. If not the case then reporting on the success of your mission)

In places you should go out of, depart from, places you should arrive at, arrive. Things that should be achieved, achieve. In addition, from places you left from, return. Throughout this a Ninja is bound to their duty until such time as they can report they have achieved a certain thing or have not achieved it. In the time that the objective has not been met, your body and your freedom are not your own. Stopping along the way for small amusements, giving playful demonstrations of your art is forbidden and strictly penalized.

This is all in line with the explanation of the 『Ninjutsu no San Gensoku The Three Principals of Ninjutsu』 in addition to the saying 『To stave off things dangerous with no harm unto him, no harm unto thyself, is the mark of *Nin no Jyō*.』 and the saying 『To stave off things dangerous with harm coming to him but no harm unto thyself, is the mark of *Nin no Chū*.』 along with the saying 『Barely escaping with harm coming to both him and thyself, is the mark of *Nin no Ge*.』 It is more than likely that my readers all have attained a firm understanding of this clear and simple *Jō-Chū-Ge* three level division to Ninjutsu. However in some situations, when it absolutely cannot be helped, Ninja must, in order to complete their duty, or must *because it is their duty*, cause injury to another and thereby place oneself in great danger.

Regardless of one's dislike this may result in you receiving an injury, yet is a task that cannot be turned town. This part...is really rather unpleasant. To be a Ninja and to fall outside the scope of the three levels of *Jō-Chū-Ge* is to be a red-faced embarrassment so total that it is like to reverberate into the next generation. As a killer would therefore be ostracized, in other words having to cut someone down, if not a case where your serious task is being impeded, then it should be avoided lest one fall into ruin. For this reason within the confines of Ninjutsu, should the situation arise where one has no choice but to cut a person, there is a particular Ninjutsu-esque method that is adhered to.

◎忍術式に定められた人の斬り方

The Ninjutsu Style and Method Designated for Cutting People

This method is used in the case whereupon a Ninja is in the midst of the enemy. Men of strength are closing in and one cannot help but be surrounded. This is an extreme measure where there is no room to maneuver and no way to apply a Jutsu. It is a last ditch effort done while being ready for death. It is neither fleeing nor concealing. The body is in full light, exposed. A witless, berserker wildly swinging attack by a novice it is not. It is instead purposely at an almost leisurely pace and to the opponent it seems *as if they are invited in*.

What happens next is fairly cheeky with its impertinence. You approach each other. He realizes that you are making no attempt to escape. Then, judging the proper time, we unexpectedly stop our movement with a last quick, determined footfall that echoes out *Pittari!* Dropping back a step the opponent, whose sword is already drawn, also plants his feet. So here we are in a state with our feet squared off not showing much concern or interest in the bared blade in front of us. In the end the scene is one where, well, there is no escape as the opponent shifts into *Dai jō dan*[1].

We, on the other hand, are relaxed and have not drawn our sword. We stand with the left half of the body forward, on an angle. The left shoulder is purposely stuck out to draw an attack. The hand of that arm grips the *Tsuba-moto*[2], or the spot just below the sword guard. As for the right hand, it hangs loosely at our side. This is seemingly mocking the opponent, as the Ninja appears to be evaluating something, searching perhaps for an unexpected method of attack. The overall atmosphere is one of hissing maliciousness. An unearthly presence seems to surround us. All in all we are an uncomfortable opponent to face. Watching the opponent's eyes we detect a 『Ki no Ugoki.』 In that instant the Ninja rapidly twists the body and here the left leg in the front position comes into play. In the interval of the 『Mabataku no ma』, we trace a half-circle, drawing it back behind us. At the same time we drop the body

---

[1] 大上段 A sword stance or Kamae where the sword is held above the head with both hands with the feeling of being ready to strike down the opponent.

[2] 鍔元

down low and plant the left knee on the ground. The right knee, which has come to the front, remains upright. Leaving no gap, the sword is drawn. Standing up we do a sweeping upward cut, catching the opponent's downward attack. If done rapidly enough, as the opponent's Katana slices the air, completely absorbed in his attack, we cut up through the right side. We move behind the fallen opponent keeping the tip of the sword firmly directed at him[1]. After observing his condition and determining that the opponent is not like to rise, we depart the scene with no *Todome*[2].

to the back of the

Leaving without finishing the opponent with a *Todome* is part of the traditional Ninja way. Considering the great responsibility they bear, they do not have the time to go through that set of movements or otherwise dawdle about the scene. Moreover, while we are engaged in that, we could be set upon by a second wave of attack. Something unexpected or unforeseen could suddenly arise, therefore, when we consider the exceptional role and duty of the Ninja, it is easy to understand why "stopping to chew the grass along the road[3]" is forbidden. All efforts must be made to extricate oneself from that situation as to more rapidly return and fulfill your main obligation. For this reason in days past when a body was discovered with sword wounds but no *Todome*, knowledgeable samurai were known to comment

"Ah, this is the work of Ninja." with a nod of the head.

Well then, I have started out explaining 『*Shoten no Jutsu*』 and then seem to have shifted over to illustrating examples where 『*Shoten no Jutsu*』 should not be used. Next the subject of the Ninja's Katana and its particularities and uses came up. That, in turn, gave way to the method by which Ninja cut people down. In the end, this discussion ran a bit long, but be that as it may, I don't feel it has been without profit. The illustrations and explanations below regarding how to cut a person are by no means exclusive. What they describe is much like the 『*Kata*[1]』

---

[1] This keeping one's attention fixed on an opponent even after having struck a final blow is referred to as Zanshin 残心 or "remaining heart" or spirit. Done to ensure your final attack was successful.

[2] Usually written 止め, or "stopping" though Itoh Sensei writes it 十々滅 "ten+ten+destroy" Finishing off a fallen foe with a final blow.

[3] 道草食ひ Michi kusa kui.

『*Kata*[1]』 found within *Kendō*. In reality the *Kata* is adapted through *Henka*[2] in order to deal with each set of circumstances. So then, within the 『Shi-U』 only one remains unexplained.

---

[1] 型 Set of movements.
[2] 變化 Variation (of a Kata).

◎忍者が人を斬るとうすろ場
合に取る逆半身の構へ圖解

第一圖

士

上段から斬り下さ
うとする敵中の勇

左の肩口を突き出
してさつ斬れとば
かりに構へる逆半
身の忍者

Illustration One:

A diagram illustrating situation where a Ninja will cut someone. The body is in a reverse half-turned away Kamae. A brave warrior attempting to cut down from *Dai-jō Dan*. A Ninja in reverse-side facing Kamae, sticking out the left shoulder as if saying "Why don't you cut?"

121

◎逆半身の構へから人を斬る段取りの圖解

敵は泳いで右の脇を拂はれる

第二圖

點描の小圓は忍者が最初左の足を踏いた所で大半閒の點線はその足を引いた道筋

忍術の現代的練習法及び現代的實用法

一〇五

Illustration Two:

A diagram illustrating cutting a person from a reverse half-turned away Kamae. The small dotted circle is the point where the left foot started, the half circle is the path the foot traces. The opponent is as if swimming as we cut up into his right armpit area.

122

忍者が刀を指し着
けて敵の動靜を覗
ふ趣

第 三 圖

點描の小圓で下の
方にあるは忍者が
膝を突いた跡、第
二の大牛圓は忍者
の左足が次に取つ
た道筋

Illustration Three:

The lower of the small dotted circles is where the Ninja had placed his knee. The second half circle is the path the Ninja's left foot took. The Ninja keeps the sword fixed on the enemy as he evaluates his condition.

縮地の術　（四有の四）

The Art of Shrinking Distance

(The Fourth of the Shi-U)

Regardless of the exaggerated name attached to it, this is something which only you yourself can carry out. It does not concern people or things other than yourself. Thus at long last we have arrived at the one in fourth position, the last of the 『Shi-U.』 One will be unable to not be startled by the new direction things take. The meaning of 『Shukuchi no Jutsu』 is described as a technique for shrinking the ground not enacting 『Hiko Jizai』 and the like so that your body can rise up to the heavens or some other wild boast. Things other than yourself — one must consider the meaning of this technique to be the shrinking of the very ground beneath your feet. Something of a puzzle isn't it? We have no choice but to toss out the scale we have been using up to this point.

So this again? We are talking about that faster method of walking? This mechanism, such as it is, has already been revealed, so that's it right?

Well, frankly, walking normally to a destination far off can consume a lot of time. Walking at a *considerably* faster face will correspondingly reduce the time, *thus the length of the road or the ground beneath your feet shrinks,* does it not? My,my,my, this is the kind of theory that is libel to make one laugh. However looking closely at 『Shukuchi no Jutsu』 and finding only a reheated 『Yoko Aruki』 makes one go,

This again? You know mocking people is just going to cause shock that inevitably leads to anger and then they will just walk away from the whole thing.

So, in response to this I will repeat, for the third time, *getting frustrated at the name it was given only shows that you do not understand it.*

I don't want to say that the crab fellow who employs this 『Yoko Aruki』 has an oversized presence within the realm of the Ninjutsu techniques carried out long ago. Rather, from the very beginning, its reach permeated and squirmed its way through the entirety of the process of building the foundation of the 『Roku Mu』 and thereby Ninjutsu. In 『Mu Kei.』 In 『Mu Seki.』 In 『Mu Sei.』 Without the slightest regard for protocol he thrusts himself into any situation. He is everywhere in every sense of the word. Though it would seem he has crammed his stomach full of it twelve times over, he somehow remains unsatisfied. Like one with a broken compass he comes creeping and crawling into even the realm of the Sennin. Are you not just a touch too greedy there crab fellow? We are all entangled by you looking for a way out! In the early years of the Bakufu Era, there was this old fellow by the name of Hikozaemon Okubo, who could obfuscate or otherwise cloud over people as if he were burning a pile of green sticks[1]. Despite being under a flag of flat out poverty, he found a way to secure a seat as a *Rō-Chu*, as a *Waka-toshiyori* in addition to positions as magistrate of this or that[2]. No matter where you went it seemed like he was already there waiting. To make a long story short, his geezer was known for shouting his opinions hither and yon, therefore should his foolishness continue or

---

[1] Okubo Tadataka (大久保 忠教) who was referred to as Okubo Hikozaemon (大久保 彦左衛門) (1560 –1639) A Samurai in the Sengoku and Edo periods. Dissatisfied with the government at the time he wrote the *Mikawa Monogatari* (三河物語) his descendants, to thereby inform them the way a warrior should live, mixed with a chronicle of the accomplishments of the Tokugawa and Okubo clans. Tadataka served with distinction at the Battle of Takatenjin Castle, taking the head of enemy general Okabe Motonobu. Later, Tokugawa Ieyasu granted Tadataka land assessed at 3,000 石 *koku*, and appointed him 槍奉行 *Yari-Bugyō* (magistrate of spears) in the Tokugawa main battle camp. In total his service stretched over the careers of the first three Tokugawa shoguns. His nichkname was "天下のご意見番 *Tenka no Go Iken Ban*" or the "biggest loudmouth under the heavens. " There are numerous anecdotes regarding him including the story wherupon those other than 旗本 *Hatamoto*, or direct retainers of the shogun were not permitted to ride in a *Koshi* 輿 or paliquin. Takada, though fairly well known, was not at that level, so he had himself carried up to the castle in a bathtub, much to the amusement of the locals no doubt.

[2] 老中 *Rō-Chu*. Member of the Shogun's council of (elder) advisors. 若年寄 Waka-toshiyori. "Young elders," those that assisted the *Rō-Chu*.

should he fall into a hole and never return is of no concern to us. The point relevant to this discussion is how this crab fellow's appearances seem to resemble the pulp novel life of the old guy Hikozaemon[1]. Well, we all probably get a bit ticklish thinking of old grandpa Hikozaemon elbowing his way around and how it compares to the crab fellow and his 『Yoko Aruki.』 More than a few overlapping points, no?

Even should you look to find fault with this train of thought, the "dawn" of sorts that arrives with having completed the Shūgyō in this 『Yoko Aruki』 method of rapidly walking is that *the evidence of its usefulness will be right before your eyes.* It is said that ninja of the past trained this extensively to the point they could cover from thirty to fifty Ri[2] in the period between dusk to sunrise as if it were nothing. The author himself tried it out and found that ten normal paces could be covered in seven or eight steps. Therefore, clearly to someone with a bit more flexibility and a bit more spring in their hips it could be as few as five or six steps, in other words half again as fast or maybe a touch more. And as it proved to not be particularly challenging, anyone could give it a try and each and every person would no doubt be able to observe its effectiveness. In a day, or in a night, speaking specifically of a longer time not a simple afternoon or evening, a road of 30 *Ri* or 50 *Ri* stretching before one, in ten days or ten nights a distance of some 300 *Ri* to 500 *Ri* can be walked. Ah, now you see. Despite all the bad-mouthing and whatnot of the 『Shukuchi no Jutusu』 you did a spark of interest has begun to form. Further, not that I enjoy talking of urinating but those that excelled at moving quickly down roads, those known for their rapid movement from one place to the next, often ate O-Musubi ^{Rice-ball} as they walked and, as a matter of course urinated as they walked along. Though you have heard me talk about this extensively, this point is also a place where the Uchiwa[3] must be raised in approval to the Yoko Aruki of Ninjutsu. All things being equal, trying to relieve yourself while walking in the usual fashion will result in one's steps becoming shorter while with 『Yoko Aruki』 and its side facing stance one is not walking into the flow

---

[1] His interactions with a fictional character, Ishhin Tasuke 一心太助 was a popular story and was made into a Kabuki play.

[2] 里 One *Ri* is equivalent to roughly 4km or 2.5 miles.

[3] 団扇 Japanese rounded fan, the non-collapsible kind. Raising the Utsuwa is kind of live signaling approval/voting.

of urine. Forward flowing urine can be avoided when one is in a sideways Kamae. Overall a method of walking that allows one to continuously increase one's speed. I must admit this last one might be a bit far-fetched.

其の三　古への忍者の練習法は餘酷烈過ぎた（下）

Chapter Three: The training undergone by Ninja of the past was unbelievably severe. (Last Part)

So then, my intention has been to offer a full explanation and dissection of the 『*Roku Mu*』 which begins the building of our foundation and proceeds on to and joins with the middle section, the 『*Shi-U*』 encompassing full-on Ninjutsu. Next we will proceed unerringly <small>without error</small> to the actual application of Ninjutsu. At long last we may humbly lay our eyes on the exalted 『五遁 *Go Ton* Five Escapes.』

木遁 *Moku Ton* Tree Escapes

(Using Trees in Order to Erase One's Presence)

火遁 *Ka Ton* Fire Escapes

(Using Fire in Order to Erase One's Presence)

土遁 *Do Ton* Ground Escapes

(Using Earth in Order to Erase One's Presence)

金遁 *Kon Ton* Metal Escapes

(Using Metal in Order to Erase One's Presence)

水遁 *Sui Ton* Water Escapes

(Using Water in Order to Erase One's Presence)

These five are known as the 『Go Ton』 Based on the 『Go Gyo』 or the Moku-Ka-Kon-Sui used by *Inyō* Practitioners[1]. Originally,

---

[1] 陰陽家 *Inyōka* A priest/diviner or maybe even a kind of Taoist sorcerer who use Yin and Yang and the five elements for divination.

as you might suspect, the playful foolishness of the Sennin of China comes into play. In the long past *San-Goku* Era (1700 years ago) there was a particularly wicked Sennin by the name of Saji, who often made use of 『*Goton no Jutsu.*』 It is said he often made swords fly through the air and chop peoples' heads off. This is quite clearly turning one's back on the 『*San Gensoku*』 formulated by Japanese Ninjutsu, completely derailing from the *Jō-Chū-Ge* scale. Ninja of our country would never bring such disgrace upon themselves as these prankster Sennin. At any rate, this thing called 『*Go Ton no Jutsu*』 is recorded as having originated in China. Though this seems to be some indefinite time in the hazy past, thinking of it as being during the reign of our Chuai *Tennō* will give you a point of reference[1].

Note that the 『Go Ton no Jutsu』 has both an *Omote* or Obverse and a *Ura* or Reverse. The previously mentioned five are the 『表五遁 *Omote Go Ton*』 in contrast to this, the 『裏五遁 *Ura Go Ton*』 contains the following five:

---

[1] 仲哀天皇 Emperor Chūai (148?-200?) The 14th (though possibly legendary) Emperor of Japan. The name Chūai *Tennō* was likely not used during his lifetime and the area he ruled was only a portion of Japan.

According to legend, his wife was suddenly possessed by some unknown god who promised Emperor Chūai rich lands overseas. Chūai then looked to the sea, but he could see nothing and denounced his belief in the promises of the gods. The gods were enraged by this and declared that he would die and never receive the Promised Land. Instead they would go to his conceived, unborn son. The legend then states that Chūai died soon after and his widow, Jingū, conquered the Promised Land, which is conjectured to be part of modern-day Korea.

◎人遁 Jin Ton "Human Escapes"

(Using People in Order to Erase One's Presence)

◎禽遁 *Kin Ton* "Bird Escapes"

(Using Birds in Order to Erase One's Presence)

◎獸遁 *Ju Ton* "Beast Escapes"

(Using Beasts in Order to Erase One's Presence)

◎蟲遁 *Chu Ton* "Insect Escapes"

(Using Insects/Small creatures in Order to Erase One's Presence)

◎魚遁 *Gyo Ton* "Fish Escapes"

(Using Fish in Order to Erase One's Presence)

So this *Goton! Goton!* becomes a *Jūton!*[1] The 『Ura』 part associated with the 『Go Ton』 had not been formulated in Saji's era and was gradually added in the ensuing centuries. Clearly the final polish should be attributed to the Ninja of Japan. As we embark on carrying out full-fledged Ninjutsu I would like to go over an important point that connects all ten of the *Omote* and *Ura "Ton"* Escapes. The details of each of the ten Ton techniques will be detailed in the next section, but not that these are all 『隠身遁形術 *Onshin Tonkei Jutsu*』 or, in other words, Methods by Which the Body May be Hidden or Made to Disappear. This is no different from terms like 『形を遁れる *Katachi wo Nogareru* "Escape from your shape"』 or even 『姿を消す *Sugata wo Kesu* "Erase your shape."』 It follows then that for each and every Jutsu there is a specific yet varied way to carry it out. They are all potent with the essence of the 秘伝 *Hiden* secret teachings. Therefore:

---

[1] Itoh Sensei is turning the formal name of the two *Go Ton* into a kind of repetitive sound like something bouncing down the stairs doubling and turning into a *Jūton* or Ten Ton sound.

◎ 隠身遁形の極まり手（一名奥の手）
Onshin Tonkei no Kimari Te
The Decisive Finish to the Methods by Which the Body May be Hidden
or Made to Disappear   (Also referred to as the hidden hand^{w a y})

and

◎ 隠身遁形の引き延べ
Onshin Tonkei no Hiki-Nobe
Extending through Methods by Which the Body May be Hidden or
Made to Disappear

pierce through the two of these through the whole of the Ten Ton and serve as the *Kaname*, or central point of the *Omote* and *Ura*. Looking at the 『Kimari Te』 and 『Oku no Te』 they are both as the author has worked his fingers to the bone describing in the chapter titled 『忍術の決着点は何所にあるか Where can the decisive elements of Ninjutsu be found?』   In short, it is the 『Shunkan Sayo』 of Ninjutsu which, if broken down in turn, contains none other than 『Mabataku no Hataraki.』   The 『Shunkan Sayo』 is using the color, the light in the opponent's eye to judge the^{detect} 『Ki no Ugoki.』 The body and spirit, which have been thoroughly trained and hardened, move as one with 雷光石火 *Rai-Kō-Se-Ka* speed, seizing the moment when the opponent is set to launch his attack but has not yet engaged it. Through this movement we are able to smash through the leading edge of the opponent's *Ki*, disabling the "nose" of his attack and, having demolished the inertia of the body, we use the interval to rapidly make for a line outside the realm of where his hands and feet can reach us. Even should the eyes of the opponent fall upon us, our cool demeanor will turn the tables on him. Next we have 『Hiki-Nobe』 the effect gained by employing 『*Onshin Tonkei*』 also known as 『*Sugata wo Kesu* or Erasing the Shape』 which is to enable one to endure for an extremely long period or to extend an considerable distance down the road. The two form a the core of Ninjutsu in other words. The essence of the secret Hiden teachings flow through any and all of the *Jūton* meaning that inhabits the Shūgyū of the

『Roku Mu』 as well as the 『Shi-U,』 both of which are leveraged by Ninjutsu. If they are not present then Ninjutsu cannot be present. If this is not deemed needed then the *Goton! Goton!* is also not essential.

So, at long last, we come to the portion where we can discuss the effectiveness of the 『Kimari no Te』 and 『Hiki-Nobe』 then following this up with explanations of each of the *Jūton*. First we must begin with the 『Omote Goton.』

木遁の術　（木に依って姿を消す）

Moku Ton no Jutsu The Art of Tree Escapes

(Using Trees in Order to Erase One's Form)

When speaking of using trees to erase ones shape, we are not referring to using the shade of a tree or a forest or a place where lumber is kept simply as a place to hide. If it were simply that is would be no more than a child's game, equivalent to 『隠れん坊 Kakuren-Bo』 or hide-and-seek.　We would be going around shouting out "Are you ready?" and "Not Yet!" and the like. This would be an artless Waza. "Is there anything beyond this?" is the question at hand.

Of course this is making use of trees in order to erase one's shape, but we must examine the way in which these methods of disappearing are leveraged. The tree itself must be utilized. When being attacked by the enemy. When being pursued by the enemy. Perhaps when a violent ruffian seeks to threaten you. At first there is nothing but surprise. At some point however, in the 『Mabataki no Ma』 moment when surprise leads to a sense of danger, without the slightest gap, with a *Do-san!* crashing sound, should it be lumber, should it be wooden poles, or something like boards or bundles of cordwood then *knock them over*. It could be straw bales of coal, could be large empty boxes, could be a table, a desk, a bookshelf or, if you are feeling bold, a wardrobe. Even it is one you have had for a long time. All of these are things that can be substituted for 『Moku Ton,』 Anything really, as long as it collapses with effect. Its falling will surprise people, and further the *Do-san!* boom given off will startle. Hopefully it will fall into something else along the way to give off another strange *Ba-tan!* crashing sound. Of course doors, *Shoji* paper doors and *Karakami* cheap paper walls are all valid options. A word of caution is perhaps warranted here, knocking the opponent down and crushing him should not be done. Surprising the opponent, or shifting his *Ki*, his attention elsewhere is enough. Then, not losing that 『Mabataku no Ma』 interval rapidly pull yourself away from the eyes and hands of the opponent. At this point should you be able to conceal yourself in the shadow of a stand of trees, a forest, some lumber, a mountain of cordwood or a mountain of charcoal and, in the next moment and without the slightest gap, cause your form to disappear, you will have performed a double *Moku Ton*. It is, in fact, better known as:

◎ 二重木遁 *Ni-Jū Moku Ton*

In reality things such as 『三重木遁 *San Jū Moku Ton*』 or tripled and 『四重木遁 *Yon Jū Moku Ton*』 quadrupled are possible as is using *Moku Ton* in conjunction with other *Ton* techniques. All these are possible, but the basic meaning can be understood from the example of 『二重木遁 *Ni Jū Moku Ton*.』 The issue of intermeshing different 『*Ton*』 techniques will be discussed towards the end and I plan to deal with all of them there.

So, there is a *Ton* method for directly using naturally occurring trees such as a grove or a forest. This method requires a bit of set up, but first of all we must detect the 『*Ki no Ugoki*』 wafting off the enemy. Next, we deliberately allow the opponent to see us sneak down into the shadow of a tree. This, in turn, becomes a kind of *Sasoi* or invitation to attack. The opponent then begins to proceed cautiously, carefully observing the area movement as he makes his way forward with a slow *Soro-soro* sound.

"Is he hiding in fear or is he planning something by hiding?"

This suspicion makes the whole business unpleasant. Here one must ferment a certain psychological nervousness. Understanding when he has swallowed the bait, in the moment he is beginning to try and peer down on us, we suddenly burst out with frightful power and speed. Like a lion leaping from the bush, like an angry god on a rampage. Come out like a full-fledged explosion. Depending on the situation you might let out a roar like thunder or the shrill shriek of a 五位鷺 *Goizaki* black-crowned night heron, or some other daemon-bred otherworldly holler to add to the scene. By doing this you will cause the opponent to be momentarily paralyzed as his Ki is broken. Allowing that 『*Mabataku Ma*』 to escape would be unforgivable! Permit no slip of time; dodge away like a lightning flash. If there is a forest, fly into it. Should there be nothing about, rapidly go around the tree and make off in a direction the opponent is not like to expect. This is referred to as:

◎ 虚実の木遁 *Kyo-Jitsu no Moku Ton* Using Trees with Truth-Falsehood

If we had buried ourselves in the forest in that last example then it would have been a combination of 『*Kyo-Jitsu*』 and 『*Ni-Jū*.』

Soldiers deep in the woods using a pup-tent painted the same color as the surrounding trees, or with illustrations of stooping branches. In this fashion they can avoid the prying eyes of aircraft while also using the forest as cover while observing the movements of the enemy[1]. A cleverly crafted wooded board painted up to resemble a tree-making something like a stage piece from a play—and hiding in the shadow of that. Combining this with making use of the morning mist and evening haze as they occur to steadily but slowly ebb forward with a *Guuu-!* is unequivocally the 『*Hiki-Nobe*』 of 『*Moku Ton.*』 Consider however that coloring the pup-tents the color of the surrounding grass, painting

---

[1] Camouflage became important after the increase in accuracy and rate of fire of weapons at the end of the 19th C. Despite camouflage's demonstrated value, until the 20th C., armies tended to use bright colours and bold, impressive designs. These were intended to daunt the enemy, foster unit cohesion, allow easier identification of units in the fog of war, and attract recruits. Not until these uniforms covered the bodies of men in long windrows across the battlefield was there a clear pressure for change.

In the west, smaller irregular units of scouts or rangers in the 18th century, such as the 95th Rifle Regiment, which was created during the Napoleonic War, were the first to adopt unit colours in drab shades of brown and green. They carried more accurate Baker Rifles, and engaged at a longer range, and their uniform was in stark contrast to the Line regiments scarlet tunics. The British in India in 1857 were forced by casualties to dye their red tunics to neutral tones, initially a khaki (from the Urdu word for "dusty"). Technological constraints meant that patterned camouflage uniforms were not mass manufactured during WW I. Each patterned uniform was hand-painted, and so restricted to snipers, forward artillery observers, and other exposed individuals. Wikipedia.

FYI: Soon after American forces first deployed to Afghanistan, a problem with the camouflage patterns used by the US Armed Forces became immediately apparent. Watching the daily footage of US Forces in the mountains of Afghanistan and the deserts of Iraq wearing Desert BDUs and Woodland gear and remembering that the same problem had shown up 10 years earlier in the first gulf war, we decided *good camouflage for where you are might be better than perfect camouflage for somewhere else.* http://www.subroc.jp/multicam.html

grass itself on them, or affixing grass itself to the roof and walls in addition to painting the tents the color of the ground itself, when there is no vegetation present are different. All of these examples fall under the auspices of the 『*Hiki-Nobe*』 of 『*Do Ton* Earth Escapes.』 Covering a howitzer with grasses, camouflaging tanks and armoured cars also fall into the 『*Hiki-Nobe*』 of 『*Do Ton* Earth Escapes.』

   Finally I would like to wrap up with a breakdown of the different types of 『*Moku Ton.*』

◎ 色の木遁。（木の色を利用する場合。）
Iro or Color Moku Ton

(Situations where the color of trees are used.)

◎ 形の木遁。（木の形を利用する場合。）
Katachi or Shape Moku Ton

(Situations where the shape of trees are used.)

◎ 音の木遁。（木の音を利用する場合。）
Oto or Sound Moku Ton

(Situations where the sound of trees are used.)

◎ 影の木遁。（木の影を利用する場合。）
Kage or Shadow Moku Ton

(Situations where the shadow of trees are used.)

◎ 虚実の木遁。（別趣のもの。） *Kyo-Jitsu no Moku Ton.*
(A distinct aspect)

◎ 二重の木遁。（重複のもの。） *Ni-Jū no Moku Ton.*
(Multiples)

All together this totals six varieties, though if you put your mind to it you could find others.

火遁の術　（火に依って姿を消す）

Ka Ton no Jutsu The Art of Fire Escapes

(Using Fire in Order to Erase One's Form)

Of the 『*Go Ton*』 perhaps the one with the greatest effect is 『*Ka Ton.*』 The light of fire can be used and the resulting heat can be relied on. The violent interaction of these two can be made use of. It goes without saying that this can be a highly effective tool. So then making short work of that narrow split second interval, the so called 『Shunkan Sayo』 which is, plainly, the *Kimari Te* of Ninjutsu, the *Oku no Te,* the thing that must be viewed as *the essential secret teaching.* The clear, fresh, vibrant feeling released by this 『*Ka Ton no Jutsu*』 needs to be in a prominent place visible to all. Let us now shift over and look at a general breakdown of categories. For a lot of these there will be a *Nijū* doublings but for now they are the following four:

◎ 火の光を利用する場合　Hi no Hikari wo Rioh suru Ba-ai
　　Situations Where the Light of Flame is Utilized

◎ 火の影を利用する場合 Hi no Kage wo Rioh suru Ba-ai
　　Situations Where the Shadows Cast by Flame is Utilized
◎ 火の色を利用する場合 Hi no Iro wo Rioh suru Ba-ai
　　Situations Where the Color of Flame is Utilized
◎ 火の熱を利用する場合 Hi no Netsu wo Rioh suru Ba-ai
　　Situations Where the Heat of Flame is Utilized

Next we will divide them up under a different method. Each fo these is then paired with one or more of the four categories previously introduced:

▲ Situations Where We Rely on Our Own Fire

◎ Causing Intense Flame to Lash Out from a Device You Carry as you Walk About. （光 Light)

◎ Flinging the End of a Lit Cigarette (色と熱　Color and heat)

◎ Causing Fire in a Place Where it is Unlikely to Burn out of Control (光と色 Light and Color)

▲ Situations Where Other Sources of Flame are Used

◎ Flame in a Natural Setting Used As Is. (光と影 Light and Shadow)

◎ Altering Flame in a Natural Setting (光と影と色と熱 Light, Shadow, Color and Heat)

◎ Making Use of Flame That Fortuitously Presents itself. (光と影 Light and Shadow)

◎ Using an Unexpectedly Erupting Flame (光 Light)

I think that should be enough to get us started. In 『Situations Where We Rely on Our Own Fire』 a subdivision of 『Causing Intense Flame to Lash Out from a Device You Carry as you Walk About』 Ninja of the past carried something referred to as an 『打竹 Uchidake.』 Inside a small bamboo tube was a thing resembling a pocket heater, and with it one can set fires. With this one can be ready to transfer flame to a variety of things in a multitude of situations. At the same time a kind of flash grenade could be made from a mixture of gunpowder and sulfur and carried on one's person. When the need dictated the flame could be transferred to the fuse and then, timing it carefully, the "grenade" could be thrown. While quite primitive by today's standards, in the days before gaslights, electric bulbs, neon signs and things generally being lit up, the blast of light emanated must have seemed like it was from a lightning bolt, causing people to shut their eyes against it. Here, a Ninja can disappear or dissolve away in a flawless 『Mabataku ma no Hataraki.』

In today's world with matches and the like there is no need for a tool with which to carry about a burning coal. While a flash grenade can be useful a match with its simple but effective magnesium tip can, with a bit of Kufū cause an equivalent effect. Its compact size means it can be carried about in the breast pocket of one's suit without endangering ourselves. It can be whipped out, struck and tossed with a rapid shout of Sore! at any time. At the same time, the light emitted will flash out to a hundred, a thousand pairs of eyes. No doubt with this all manner of

138

splendid Ninjutsu can be conducted in the modern world. An example of sorts of this "taking hold of a chance" can be found in the masterpiece by the name of The Hakken Den[1]. Despite the youngest grandchild Tosetsu Inuyama appearing in the Koshinzuka in the town of Sugano in Toyoshima ward, no news of *Ka Ton Jutsu* being used was reported. The reason for this is perhaps that though they possess the tools, modern day people show no interest in and indeed have given up on the Shūgyō of the Ninjutsu in the long distant past.

Next we have 『Flinging the End of a Lit Cigarette.』 In this case, we are amongst the enemy as it were and one of those sharp-witted ones is able to determine that we are Ninja. Despite this he begins to close in, looking for trouble. We however, maintain a nonchalant manner and continue to smoke and make as if shooting the breeze. With a practiced puff we blow the heated ember from the end of the cigarette, striking the opponent in the area between the eyes and nose. This will catch the opponent completely off guard and will throw him into utter confusion. At the very least he will have to turn his head to dodge it and thus you will have a breakdown of his attack. Rapidly use the 『Mabataku ma no Hataraki』 to remove one's body and safely and smoothly separate oneself from danger. In addition to this, were the people of this day and age to borrow these self-defense mechanisms of Ninjutsu, in that same situation the 『Shunkan Sayo』 gained from 『Ka Ton』 could be one order of magnitude more deftly done. The Japanese of past eras with their metal tipped *Kiseru*[2] pipes could not have, in their wildest dreams

---

[1] Nansō Satomi Hakkenden 南總里見八犬傳 The Eight Dog Chronicles

106 volume epic novel by Kyokutei Bakin set in the Sengoku Era. The author went blind before finishing and dictated the last chapters to his daughter. Hakkenden is the story of eight samurai half-brothers--all of them descended from a dog and bearing the word "dog" in their surnames--and their adventures, with themes of loyalty and family honor, as well as Confucianism, Bushido and Buddhist philosophy. There is a scene where one of the brothers uses a spark given off by an opponent's sword striking a rock in order to escape. The setting was what is in modern day Toyoshima Ward. This is a joke of sorts I suppose.

[2] 煙管 The term *Kiseru*, written "smoke+pipe" originates from the Khmer word "ksher." A wooden or bamboo shaft connects a metal

envisioned such a thing. One is unlikely to find a handier convenience.
Think of the way in which a those rather unkempt fellows one sees about
dragging on a cigarette, whether they be Shikijima or Asahi, until half its
length is smoldering, then flicking it with their practiced fingertips[1]. A
brilliant coal strikes right between the eyes and then tumbles down the
face. Immediately the opponent's 『Boei Honnō』 is activated—this has
nothing to do with you, but note that when the opponent goes *Ah!* their
closing eyes signal a total collapse of their concentration. I am in no way
trying to inflate the importance of it, as with the unequivocal success of
Dousetsu Inuyama, through which can we not confirm the 『*Kimari Te*』
of 『*Ka Ton no Jutsu?*』   Differing from what we had before with the
gunpowder flare, here it is the color of flame and the heat rather than the
light that comes into play.

From there we have 『Causing Fire in a Place Where it is Unlikely to
Burn out of Control』 whereupon having slipped inside the enemy's
castle or manor un-noticed, we sense it is the appropriate time. So then,
maybe, in the corner of the garden or in the space between trees? In the
shade of one of those large stones in the garden or between *Dozō*[2]
storehouses? At any rate, the main objective being to draw the eyes of
people. Wherever the fire is set, the Ninja were strictly against arbitrarily
starting fires that could rage out of control. Following this edict prevents
them from having anything to regret[3]. Fallen leaves are gathered, or
scraps of grass, scraps of paper, sawdust and other flammable grasses are
lit with the aforementioned *Uchidake*. And then suddenly, with a *Baah!*
sound. From the midst of darkness fingers of flame begin to rise. The

---

mouth piece to the bowl.

[1] 敷島 *Shikijima* cigarettes were around from 1904-1943. At one point
they were so popular that the company ran short of tobacco.

朝日 Asahi was an unfiltered cigarette brand that was around from 1904-
1976, smoked by luminaries such as Natsume Soseki.

[2] 土蔵 A storehouse with a design common all over Japan with only
minor variations. A basic wood-framed, plaster-walled, tiled-roof served
to maintain a stable temperature and humidity year-round.
[3] Fires could spread quickly amonst tightly packed wood and paper
houses and the death penalty for setting fires was common.

effect of the color of this flame, the light of this flame is that the enemy troops nearest come virtually tumbling over each other without so much as a "by your leave." That they will come racing to gather there is all but inevitable. At this point we do not allow the slightest gap and make our move in a direction where enemy is least expecting it. Using the 『Kimari Te』 of 『Onshin Ton Kei』 while at the same time using the effect of the 『Roku Mu/Shi-U』 to affect our 『Hiki-Nobe.』

All the above involves techniques the Ninja can apply at will, without struggle. Though it is often said of Ninja 『忍者は獨往獨來を旨とす。 Ninja in principal appear on their own and depart on their own.』 the fact of the matter is 『二人の忍 Futari no Nin Two Ninja Working in Unison』 as well as 『三人の忍 San-nin no Nin Three Ninja Working in Unison』 do exist. In the past it was known that up to three Ninja would be involved in infiltrations[1]. Thus while one was causing tongues of flame to rise up, the other one, or two, can continue on to their task in a line straight as an Ichi Mon Ji[2]. Strategies involving 『Futari no Nin』 as well as 『San-nin no Nin』 can be very effective, but this is not limited only when withdrawing. As mentioned before, when driving in at the target it can also be useful. In Ninjutsu this is referred to as 『虚実の転換 Kyo-Jitsu no Tenkan The Switch Between Truth and Fasehood.』

Next we will examine the topic of 『Flame in a Natural Setting Used As Is』 under the heading of 『Situations Where Other Sources of Flame are Used.』 These include things such as Jyōyatō[3] standing light towers, police station lanterns or lights in front of houses. Depending on the situation or how desperate the need, the light tower can be blown out or

---

[1] 『二人の忍 Futari no Nin』 and 『三人の忍 San-nin no Nin』 are discussed at length in Itoh Sensei's previous book 忍術の極意 Ninjutsu no Gokui.
[2] 一文字 The Kanji for the numeral one is a straight, horizontal line.

[3] 常夜燈

141

knocked over, causing the eyes of those accustomed to its brightness to become confused by the sudden pitch-darkness. Stealing that interval where the 『Mabataku ma no Hataraki』 occurs is of course one method. Yet another approach would be for us to step out into the light, purposely exposing ourselves. Reading the moment the enemy's gaze crystalizes on us, we leap and slip our form back into the shadows. This is a perfect use of 『Shunkan Sayo,』 and further one level of the 『Oku no Te』 of 『Onshin Ton Kei.』 This type of technique is not for the unskilled or the faint of heart. Should one be able to use both the light and the shadows in such a manner then one will certainly be in the upper ranks of Ninjutsu.

Perhaps even more so than the previous example 『Altering Flame in a Natural Setting』 is a fundamental technique. The thing that differs about this one is that we are not simply blowing out or toppling over a lantern. Should there be a *Jyōyatō*, then suddenly block its light, changing the direction of the light. If it is something that can be borne easily then change the place it sits or hangs. In short, alter the way the area is lit. By doing this the light and shadow move and change violently, and those that have grown used to the environment are thrown into tumult. In the ensuing 『Mabataki no Ma』 waste no time in rapidly conducting the technique that needs to be done. Further, in the case of a *Hibachi* or *Irori*, paper, wood shavings, some sort of grass that will flame up quickly or other such material can be deftly whipped into the flames causing them to flare up with a *Bouu*! sound[1]. Another possibility is making use of a *Tetsubin*[2] with water at a full boil. Suddenly flipping this over will result in a fantastic billowing cloud of ash and smoke being erupted. Clearly to one must operate with Den-Kō-Se-Ka speed in order to fully realize this chance. Note that here, with regards to how to categorize this with regards to the 『Go Ton,』 that while the term 『Kiri-

---

[1] 火鉢 *Hibachi*    囲爐裏 *Irori*  Both of these are charcoal grill/stoves though the Hibachi can be of any shape while the Irori is more or less part of the house.

[2] 鉄瓶 Your standard iron tea pot.

fog-*Gakure Jutsu*』 was not mentioned, this is a combination of both 『Ka Ton』 and 『Do Ton.』 It is the effect of 『Ka Ton』 that called up our rather impressive cloud of ash, while conversely, taking a look at this from the perspective of 『*Kiri Gakure,*』 the flame contained in the ash is certainly 『*Ka Ton*』 while the ash that does not contain flame is 『*Do Ton.*』 Concerning making use of the flame elements around a *Hibachi* or *Irori*, one is that the *Hibashi*[1] fire tongs can be used to fling blazing coals around, while another possibility is for us to kick over a Hibachi, sending sparks and coals hither and yon. This kind of application is sort of ham-fisted and not suited to the upper echelons of Ninjutsu. Again the above is used primarily in extreme cases when beset upon by an enemy and thus we aim to kick the flames into their eyes. For situations like this the issue of upper or lower with regards to the level of Ninjutsu does not, of course, apply. *Hikari to Kage to Iro to Netsu.* Light and Shadow, Color and Heat. These are all elements of this chapter.

The next one is 『Making Use of Flame That Fortuitously Presents itself』 where a fire is burning by happenstance along the path a Ninja is proceeding down. Sometimes these fires will have people attending to them, other times as with *Kakaribi* there will be no one about[2]. Both of these situations can be made use of. After a *Matsuri* or other festival that can run late into the night, here and there *Chochin* can be left hanging from the eves of houses. The hand held *Chochin* carried by persons moving down the road at night are also valid[3]. There are other possibilities as well. Chancing upon a *Jyōyatō*, a farmer's pile of

---

[1] 火箸 Long metal chopsticks used for mucking about with charcoal.

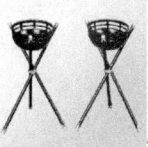

[2] 係火 Somewhat akin to modern-day streetlights, they lined the sides of major roads/buildings. People would usually be set to watch a series of them rather than one for each.

[3] 提燈 Chochin come in a variety of sizes and shapes from hand-held jobs to the one in front of Asakusa's *Sensoji* 浅草寺 Temple that is like 12 feet tall.

smoldering rubbish or a burning pile of kindling. Each and all are associated with this category. Though the different uses of the light and shadow of fire the 『Mabataku ma no Hataraki』 can be leveraged and thereby the 『Onshin Ton Kei』 which flows through the whole of it. If looking at them separately then one could suddenly kick a pile of burning kindling up in a wide arc, stamp it out or, in the case of a Chochin, simply knock it over, suddenly shifting light to darkness. The border between being able to or not able to effectively shock the eyes and indeed the whole spirit of the enemy is the place where 『Ka Ton no Jutsu』 will be successfully enacted or not. In particular the kicking of the burning kindling takes a certain amount of dexterity—no ham-fistedness—if done expertly and the effect of sending the flame of the Hibachi or Irori will know no bounds. Whether it be against five people or ten people, their faces should all be bathed evenly in a wash of sparks, and as one they will turn away with a cry of Ah! And like a draught of clear water down the throat, you will make your escape.

The final one remaining to us is 『Using an Unexpectedly Erupting Flame.』 Though it is the last, this one gets the gold medal in 『Ka Ton.』 These points are absolutely the epitome of Ninjutsu. It is as if the eye of 『Go Ton』 itself were scooped from its cavity and held aloft. As in the Haiku by Buson[1] referring to those burdened with a palanquin:

A laden porter's stick

Stone clipped and sparks fly

Barren field so alive

Striking down with the steel tipped Ishizuki[2] of the staff, they

---

[1] 与謝蕪村 Yosa Buson (1716- 1784). One of the great names in Haiku poetry as well as a painter famous for his use of "...the colloquial language to transcend colloquialism." Feeling that contemporary poets had lost 独創性 creativity and ingenuity he urged a "蕉風回帰 Return to Basho" referring to Matsuo Bashō 松尾芭蕉(1644 –1694) who was the most famous poet of the Edo Era.

[2] 石附 The metal or stone end of a walking stick to lessen the wear. Also

inadvertently hit rock and due to the surrounding darkness, the flame stands out vibrantly. If this were the *Ishizuki* of a *Yari* or spear then it would no doubt be more impressive. Another possibility includes the sparks that pop off charcoal from time to time, bursting out like fireworks. However unexpected that momentary flame may be, it cannot be allowed to slip through your fingers. In the end it is likely that only the trained, hardened Ninja can fully harness that one flash of one second. Our body's movement will of course be coupled with a sharp and
sensitive mind with both operating working in unison.

"But let's look at this practically," they say "No matter how adept the Ninja, being able to react to and make use of the light from an unexpected burst of flame is almost beyond reason! First of all it's highly unlikely that such a thing would occur at a time when it could be of use! I mean...more than unlikely it would never happen!"

Alright. Please listen. As this readiness to react is part of their everyday training, a fundamental ability if you will, *it is only the opponent who is caught unprepared.* The Ninja craft a situation where *they* are the ones who are not caught out.

All of the above takes place when one is cornered in a near hopeless situation and on the verge of 「*Nin no Yabure.*」 it is the only Waza left at a time when aggressive opponents are flinging themselves at you fully, with flashing blades drawn. As our life is on the line it is inevitable that we must face them. In the midst of all of this, however the before mentioned 「*San Gensoku*」 that illuminate Ninjutsu must be strictly adhered to while, at the same time, the heavy burden that is the need to achieve success in our duty permits us neither to cut or be cut. To the upmost of our ability we must refrain from using the Ninja-esque method of cutting people with our sword and, instead, focus on slipping away and withdrawing with a *Suru-ri* sliding sound.

With this mindset firmly in place, any high-level Ninja, should any be present, are now no doubt nodding ever so slightly to themselves,

"It is we who will launch a ferocious attack. With every fiber of our being we will begin to violently cut into them."

This is however, all for effect. The fact of the matter is our intent is to

---

the counterweight on the end of a spear.

strike the opponent's blade forcefully with our own. Should the strikes be done skillfully then the eyes will be startled by a spray of *Hanabi* fireworks. We however, having planned this, are in no way surprised and thus it is only the enemy who is flummoxed. To add insult to injury, as it were, if the strikes are expertly done, then the Hanabi from the blade will drift like flower petals into the opponent's eyes. Our chance is the second they react with a *Haah!* sound. Next, of course, is what we have been waiting for: rapidly using the 『*Kimari Te*』 of 『*Onshin Ton Kei.*』

Looking at this again, we, for our part, hardly lift a finger, rather it is the opponent who is left struggling with an invisible enemy, doing Sumō alone as it were[1]. We, however, launched flame from our blade at them, taking them completely off guard.

This next method which follows the last is a rather ironic one. It takes into account how Ninja have adjusted their eyes to the darkness to a degree that they are much like an owl. Under duress as above we first determine, where a very large rock is sticking up out of the earth. Then in order to gradually lure the opponent in that direction, we shift our body rapidly as if intent on avoiding the drawn blade of the enemy. The enemy obediently follows us. At last, in front of the rock we plant our feet as if saying

"Well, then come on!"

We adopt a *Kamae* that invites the opponent in, while at the same time leaving our *Katana* in its *Saya*. The enemy is going to take this as an insult and become enraged.

"This bastard trickster...Im going to cut him clean in half!"

This is the second which we have been preparing for. In a flash the Ninja is gone, not wasting this chance. The tip of the blade we dodged strikes down forcefully and quite unexpectedly on the boulder. In the moment of realization that comes with *"Hah?!"* it is already too late. An inexplicable torrent of *Hanabi* strikes and overwhelms the eyes. For a split second they wince and go Ah! That is the moment the Ninja scoop up and use it to leap into the darkness. The enemy gets his head straightened out and looks at the place that *bastard trickster* was.

---

[1] 独り相撲 Hitori-zumō.(lit. Doing Sumō alone) Tilting at or fighting windmills.

He's gone!

"What!? He's vanished?" he says to himself flummoxed.

What happened here is that the opponent's 『*Honō Sayo*』 natural defenses were doubly utilized in the 『*Kimari no Te.*』 This is referring to causing a fighter to become enraged as, under normal circumstances, when calm, even at night one would hardly fail to notice a large boulder. Speaking of caution in general, this differs from the situation before where blades were smashing into each other. This ironic method does have the weak point of being ineffective against someone of a careful nature.

This brings us to the end of the definition and explanation of 『Ka Ton.』 There is another one that would seem at first to be associated with 『Ka Ton』 is in fact under the umbrella of 『Kon Ton.』 It is an exceedingly unusual Waza but we will discuss it in another chapter.

火遁の術の圖解二種

其一
發光彈を
投げ出し
た場合

Illustrations of two varieties of Ka Ton no Jutsu

Number 1: Situation where a flash grenade is thrown.

其二
敵の刃を
石に切り
着けさせ
た場合

Number 2: Situation where the opponent's blade strikes a rock.

土遁の術　（土に依って姿を消す）

Do Ton no Jutsu The Art of Earth Escapes

(Using Earth in Order to Erase One's Form)

There is nothing more plentiful on the Earth than the spaces covered by soil. There is no ground wider than that which is made up of soil and as there is nothing as easy to use as soil 『Do Ton no Jutsu』 thereby has innumerable applications. Just to clarify, this is not referring to looking down upon the Earth from above, as it is covered by vastly more water than land. What is being noted is the fact that the vast majority of humanity resides upon the ground. Please do not misinterpret this for some anti-geographic sciences argument. First let us line up the various divisions of 『*Do Ton no Jutsu.*』 Within Ninjutsu, basically all things that grow from the ground, with the exception of trees but including varieties of grasses, moss as well as bamboo and scraps left over from harvesting rice and such are all counted as a resource for 『*Do Ton.*』 Just a moment there. Resist the temptation to scoff at moss being of use for 『*Onshin Ton Kei.*』 Of the rocks that cover the earth, there are some that are completely overgrown with moss and some that are naked. Wouldn't the way each is used be different? The rocks that were previously spoken of, whether large or small, are also clearly, materials for 『Do Ton.』 Sand would thereby fall into the same category. Fog, mist or haze rising from the earth as well as rain, sleet and snow absorbed by it are classified in this category as well. Severely frosted ground. Ice and its transformed state the icicle. Frost tendrils and so on and so on. None of the above can be excluded from use in 『*Do Ton.*』 As I promised originally I will now break down this as well in accordance with the 『*Go Ton,*』 therefore it includes: the color of the sky and its variations, and everything from the sun, moon, stars, clouds and rainbows to thunder and lightning and so on... All of the above are crammed, somewhat unwillingly into this chapter on 『*Do Ton.*』 At any rate let us separate these things according to the situation where they will be used.

◎ 土の形を利用する場合 *Tsuchi no Katachi wo Riyo suru Ba-ai.* Situations Where the Shape of the Ground is Used.

◎ 土の色を利用する場合 *Tsuchi no Iro wo Riyo suru Ba-ai.*

Situations Where the Color of the Ground is Used.

◎ 土の質を利用する場合 *Tsuchi no Shitsu wo Riyo suru Ba-ai.*
Situations Where the Nature of the Ground is Used.

◎ 土の力を利用する場合 *Tsuchi no Chikara wo Riyo suru Ba-ai.*
Situations Where the Power of the Ground is Used.

◎ 土の味を利用する場合 *Tsuchi no Aji wo Riyo suru Ba-ai.*
Situations Where the Flavor of the Ground is Used.

◎ 土の属を利用する場合 *Tsuchi no Zoku wo Riyo suru Ba-ai.*
Situations Where the Association With the Ground is Used.

With just these six categories the above represents somewhat of an abbreviated list. First of all, taking a look at 『Situations Where the Shape of the Ground is Used』 depressions or protuberances in the ground, slopes, ridges between rice paddies, collapsed hillsides, the incline of a mountain, stone steps, large ornamental rocks, naturally occurring stones, piles of rocks, piles of gravel, piles of sand, mounds of soil, *Sekitō* stone towers[1] and so on. All can be called into play depending upon ones needs when seeking to enact 『*Mabataku Ma no Hataraki*』 or as an aid to its effect. In this situation it is the 『*Hiki-Nobe*』 of 『*Onshin Ton Kei*』 rather than the 『*Kimari Te*』 that is employed. In other words we are either using or relying on things that are immobile or things that do not stand out. At this point I would like to add a word of caution: Whether a vertical cave or a horizontal cave, earthen holes or stone holes or anything resembling such should not be entered. Crawling into caves is strictly forbidden for Ninja and is referred to as 『鬼窟に生なし *Kikutsu ni Iki nashi* No escape from the Devil's lair.』 If it is something that clearly has an exit like a tunnel then you are fine[2].

As for the next one, 『Situations Where the Color of the Ground is Used』 we have to change the way in which we explain things. This is

---

[1] 石塔 They come in a variety of layers and styles.
[2] This seems to be a bit of a joke as Itoh Sensei uses the English word "tunnel."

does not imply that we will have to separate red earth from black, blue earth from white and all the myriad colors in between. What this means is that at night nearly all earth appears to be black, therefore we can simply use the soil available at the time to color ourselves. Becoming the same as night enables us to better erase our shape and melt into the darkness, becoming just another one of the multiple shades of black or something that merges with black. This too is similar to the previous one where as it is embedded with a larger percentage of 『Hiki-Nobe』 rather than the 『Kimari Te.』

On the other hand, with 『Situations Where the Nature of the Ground are Used』 we, at long last, make use of the 『Kimari Te』 of 『Do Ton.』 This will not consist of some fussy geologic breakdown but rather we will, simply, use the 『Mabataku Ma』 Waza in situations to withdraw, whether it be a fortuitous pile of dirt by your hand, sand or a rock snatched up and in an instant flung at the enemy. Things to consider range from soil that if gripped immediately forms a hard ball, or if gripped does not immediately form a hard ball. A clod that is half-formed can be flung at the enemy to open and spread out, while things like a rock are solid to begin with. In short, all the perambulations and all the qualities of the things that exist within 『Do Ton』 must be evaluated. Though this has been stated, I would like to re-iterate that one must have an understanding of the nature of each and every one of these and how its use changes. Ones that can be used as *Metsubushi*[1], things that will cause pain, things that will cause surprise...each according to its own use. By doing this when they finds themselves in a tight spot, the thorough training regiment, namely the Ninja's Shūgyō in 『Do Ton no Jutsu』 allows Ninja to employ them without error. It follows then that by doing this we can understand the strengths and weaknesses of 『Do Ton no Jutsu』 as those amongst the Ninja do. So then, the theory that was put forth when we discussed 『Do Ton』 applies here as well. Should we utilize not only the 『Kimari Te』 of throwing a clod of earth to resolve a situation, but also use the color or shape of the earth in order to cause ourselves to "disappear" in order to distance ourselves from the opponent, then this is referred to as:

二重の土遁 *Nijū no Doton* Doubled Do Ton

---

[1] 目潰し Blinding powder.

If we look at this according to the divisions of the 『Go Ton』 then 『Kiri Gakure no Jutsu The Art of Fog Escapes』 is, as I have already alluded to within both 『Ka Ton』 and 『Do Ton.』 Though associated with 『Do Ton』 and while there is no apparent connection between fire and 『Kiri Gakure no Jutsu,』 Ninja of the past typically walked about with a pouch containing the ash of oyster shells and powdered lime. In this manner when exposed to danger a fistful can be taken up and thrown in the opponent's face while we can leap away and escape as we see fit.

This is, according to the divisions of the 『Go Ton』 is the very definition of 『Situations Where the Nature of the Ground is Used.』 Consider, if you will, the degree to which the modern sciences have evolved, we now have the searing heat belched forth by strong hydrochloric acid and the chill belched forth by strong ammonia. These could be soaked into separate batches of sawdust and placed in separate bags that can withstand the extremely acidic or basic mixture. Ensuring that they are secured firmly as to not allow any hint of their presence to be detected, they can be fitted as to allow their quick opening. With the pouches tied to either side of the waist they can be carried about. Should the need arise, they both can be picked off and flung together in mid-air so that something that is neither smoke nor ash but indeed a real and true fog will erupt. When one flings ash or some such, the opponent's main worry is some of it getting in their eyes, I can't even imagine how superior this method is. And on a final note, I would like to mention the smoke screens used during wartime[1]. One would be hard pressed to argue that these are not large scale applications of Ninjutsu. I think it would not be too presumptuous to place these in the 『Situations Where the Nature of the Ground are Used』 of 『Do Ton no Jutsu.』

Next we will look at 『Situations Where the Power of the Ground is Used.』 This too makes use of the 『Kimari no Te』 of 『Mabataku Ma』

---

[1] Warships have sometimes used a simple variation of the smoke generator, by injecting fuel oil directly into the smoke stack. An even simpler method that was used in the days of steam-propelled warships was to restrict the supply of air to the boiler. This resulted in incomplete combustion of the coal or oil, which produced a thick black smoke. Because the smoke was black, it absorbed heat from the sun and tended to rise above the water. Therefore navies turned to various chemicals, such as titanium tetrachloride, that produce a white, low-lying cloud. Wikipedia.

with earth. Though we used the word 『Power』 it does not mean that this level has a particularly complex theory associated with it. Indeed many people will no doubt recall the line from Sun Tzu's <u>Art of War</u> 『圓石を千仭の山より転がすが如き ...*the momentum of a round stone rolled down a mountain into a valley a thousand fathoms below.* [1]』 In other words, in that exact situation or even in one similar, finding a giant boulder or, if available one bigger, and rolling it down from atop a slope or down the sides of a mountain. When the enemy's "Liver is crushed[2]" riding in on that wave of disarray and, leaving not the slightest interval, employing that thing we so often talk about. It goes without saying that the dual hare is not to crush the enemy to death.

Now the next one we have to look at is 『Situations Where the Flavor of the Ground is Used.』 Though there may be a somewhat different approach within "flavor," when one understands what is meant by this "*Aji.*" It is to what degree the soil is crumbly and dry making a *Basa-basa* sound. It is to what degree the soil is sticky with a *Neto-neto* sound or muddy with a *Doro-doro* sound. It includes everything from the sensation of the ground, the ways in which it can be utilized to the degree to which it will be a hindrance. This is, in other words, what is meant by the 『*Aji* or flavor.』 Therefore this division links together both the 『*Kimari Te*』 and 『*Hiki-Nobe*』 of the 『*Mabataku ma no Hataraki*』 in a kind of reciprocating union.

The key to all this is that by understanding 『*Aji*』 of the various types of soil, when cornered or in a tight spot the manner in which it can be used will be apparent. So in situations where we are trying to withdraw that knowledge is going to give rise to solutions using the above varieties. To give just a couple of quick examples, dried and parched earth can easily stand in for ash as a Metsubushi. In the case of wet earth

---

[1] This is part of a section in Chapter 5, which deals with the energy/inertia/momentum in one's army:

> *Thus the energy developed by good fighting men is as the momentum of a round stone rolled down a mountain into a valley a thousand fathoms below.*

[2] 肝を潰す *Kimo wo tsubusu.* Crush the liver or organs in general. Destroy the fighting spirit.

or clay according to the strength of its stickiness or how it pulls apart, they can quickly be compacted and thrown at the opponent's face or anywhere that may seem vital. This last is clearly 「Kimari Te.」 Should then one come upon a muddy patch whilst being pursued, lure the enemy there to slip and tumble about while you remain stable. These cannot be classified as anything other than 「Hiki-Nobe.」

There is still one more. It is referred to as 「Situations Where the Association With the Ground is Used.」 Please don't feel that this 「Zoku」 is going to be more difficult to comprehend than 「Aji.」 It is simply that with regards to illustrating elements within the field of Ninjutsu it can often be difficult to craft an explanation that will allow understanding to come quickly. Trust that I am not purposely trying to complicate things here. With the exception of the trees used in 「Moku Ton no Jutsu」 anything that grows from the ground including grasses, including mosses, including bamboo, including scraps from rice fields and even things that do not spring from the earth. Snow, hail, frost and ice to frost tendrils poking up from the ground. Phenomena such as fog, mist, haze and, while it might seem wildly presumptuous as the sky is next to the earth, the sun itself the stars themselves, the clouds themselves, he rainbows themselves, thunder itself, lightning itself and all the things that are encompassed by the thing called *Sora* or sky are, despite any departure from reason or doubt are associated wholly and absolutely with the earth. It is, in fact, *because of this seemingly disordered mix* that 「Association With the Ground」 is so exceptional.

This 「Association With the Ground」 is rather energetic is it not? Adopting all the elements of 「Association With the Ground」 almost casually— please here take a moment to marvel at the sheer force of will possessed by the Ninja of the past—this boundless limitless thing that Ninjutsu uses as raw materials for its purposes, leaving nothing unused. While it might seem necessary then to pick apart each, one at a time and examine and dissect it, I am not sure if that would result in pleasure or pain. At any rate, it seems I have spent a bit too much time on the first ones and sort of went on and on with a *Dara-dara* lanquidity. But fear not, as many elements would overlap, I suppose my dear friends and readers might become a bit bored with it all. Rest assured, one can review the points covered in the other five and it is my hope you can come to discern the points where they perfectly overlap. Now we will proceed on to 「Kon Ton.」

金遁の術　（金に依って姿を消す）

Kon Ton no Jutsu　The Art of Metal Escapes
(Using Metal in Order to Erase One's Form)

While perhaps the techniques in the neighbouring topic 『Do Ton』 were somewhat chaotic and difficult to distinguish from one another, in 『Kon Ton』 conversely you will find to be snug and compact. Overall they will wrap up rather neatly in the end. The varieties of 『Kon Ton』 are:

◎ 金属及び金属製品の光を利用する場合。
Kinzoku oyobi Kinzoku Seihin no Hikari wo Riyo suru Ba-ai.
Situations where the Light Given off by Metal or Metal Objects are Used

◎ 金属及び金属製品の音を利用する場合。
Kinzoku oyobi Kinzoku Seihin no Oto wo Riyo suru Ba-ai.
Situations where the Sound Given off by Metal or Metal Objects are Used

Come hell or high water, for the 『Kimari no Te』 of 『Onshin Ton Kei』 these are the only two categories that I am going to lay out. Should I try to cram in others to the list, it would likely only result in immediate confusion. As it is so compact, some aspects and some of the 『Aji』 differ markedly from those already presented, and it is this very incense that we seek to savor.

Taking a look at the issue brought up by the first one 『Situations where the Light Given off by Metal or Metal Objects are Used.』 Note that the light from any object made of metal can be of use in Ninjutsu. Unfortunately with regards to situations like this I have to report that they are more or less non-existent.

As you are well aware polished metals tend to gleam in the light. In the daytime they reflect the sun and at night it is the light of the moon or *Jyōyatō,* standing lantern, that is reflected back. Though the possibility of dazzling an opponent's eyes with these rays of light would seem to be the epitome of something used in Ninjutsu, the fact of the matter is something that could affect the eyes in such a manner would be heavy, hard and moreover a bulky object. First of all, and this is probably the death knell for this, is that it would not be at all in line with the way Ninja equip themselves. I will lay out the whole package for you here.

Amongst the Ninja a rather simple, even austere manner was
^{esteemed}
valued. This is going to seem a bit like lining up two varieties of antique
Katana and comparing the Tsuba. By say, running our eyes across them,
one of them—rather one variety of them— is not for killing nor is it for
sparring. The fact of the matter it is something utterly flawless and
genuine that takes the absolute center. It is the 『*Mabataki no Ma,*』 ^{center stage}
defined as the moment when an enemy has formulated his attack but is
within the infinitesimally small interval before the attack is engaged, we
^{instantaneously}
suddenly react with Den-Ko-Se-Ka speed. The Katana at our hip flies
out like a rush of wind and flash it across the eyes in a blur that seems to
trace an arc of frost. Nothing but a white flash across the eyes. The
sharpness of that light and the speed with which it appears will cause the
opponent to falter with a Hah! gasp of surprise. Then the ring of the
Tsubanari is heard, though the hand has moved too fast to for the eye to
follow the *Nōtō* sheathing of the sword. Leaping with a sudden burst as if
a Tengu, we are gone in this 『Kimari Te.[1]』 Manipulating a situation
with this level of refinement is well beyond all but Ninja of the highest
level. Though we did not vie the last Jutsu much of a chance, in this next
variety we will present something quite singular. The Ninja of the past,
seeking to make the most out of 『Kon Ton,』 placed in their breast
pocket a small round mirror polished brighter than the *Jūgoya* Full
moon.[2] It can be carried about as if it were a shadow above our hearts. It
goes without saying that this was a mirror made of metal. In the long

---

[1] 天狗 Representations of the *Tengu* vary wildly, but it usually appears
to be half man/half bird (hence they are often referenced when
describing someone hopping around quickly) often with a red face and
long nose. Though they are 妖怪 yokai (monster-spirits) they are
sometimes worshipped in Shinto.   Also:

Buddhism long held that the Tengu were disruptive demons and
harbingers of war. Their image gradually softened, however, into one
of protective, if still dangerous, spirits of the mountains and forests.
Tengu are associated with the ascetic practice known as 修験道
Shugendō, and they are usually depicted in the distinctive garb of its
followers, the 山伏 *Yamabushi. Wikipedia.*

[2] 十五夜 The full moon according to the traditional Chinese calendar the
15th day of the month.

past era of Ninjutsu, clearly glass mirrors were not commonplace. In place of that they had 『Kon Ton』 and there was no such thing as some strangely names 『Glass Ton[1].』

So then, a Ninja has fallen prey to bad luck and has been cornered, with little or no chance to escape. Fortunately amongst the enemy someone is carrying a *Chochin*. A fortuitous *Jyōyatō* behind them or an open flame somewhere can also be used in a pinch. Even should the black letters standing out on the *Chochin* spell *Go Yō*, we needn't worry[2]. Due to the rays of light from the enemy's side shooting at us, glittering with a *Kirin-kirin* sound, our pupils are sure to be gushing over, fixing us as if platinum arrows had been shot from a bow. That same arrow that is flashing through the night, aimed at us—here it is as if a chance has been given to us by a *Kami,* or a God, is utilized. Without missing a beat we raise our mirror and play the light from the flame about the enemy and everything goes topsy-turvy as we are the ones piercing their pupils.

"Wait just a minute there! It is not as if someone has just set off a magnesium flare in that era of no light bulbs or gaslights where the night was as dark as a nightmare. Just sort of casting back the light is not going to have any great effect, I man who wasn't accustomed to the night like an owl back then? If someone were to get done in by a little flash of light in the eye they would be the laughing stock."

This is absolutely true. The folks that lived in the past were all well accustomed to a deep dark night and therefore even rather feeble light flashed in an artless fashion would leave them spellbound. In that second the Ninja vanishes. In this situation the enemy begins flashing their light around haphazardly while the Ninja, and this will have many nodding in agreement, only reflects back the light required for their methods.

Moving a bit onward from that point, there is a certain time when the Ninja will purposely reveal themselves in broad daylight, sun glowing on all sides. Completely exposed. This is the situation where we are faced with anywhere from one to several people, we skillfully hold a mirror above our heads and fire an arrow of light, burning through all the

---

[1] 玻璃 Itoh Sensei uses the characters for quartz with an English reading of "glass" above them.
[2] 御用 "Official Business." These Kanji were written on *Chochin* lanterns that the police carried around.

eyes before it.

Looking back on our discussion, 『Ka Ton no Jutsu』 has been thoroughly gone over though, but, in fact, this thing that might appear at first to belong to 『Ka Ton』 is actually a part of 『Kon Ton.』 These somewhat unusual Waza we have just scratched the surface are all make use of this pocket mirror. This metal mirror plays quite a central role. I will now present the other half of the *Wari-fu*[1].

The second is 『Situations where the Sound Given off by Metal or Metal Objects are Used.』 For this things on your person will not be used. Interestingly when compared to 『Light』 we are dropping down several ranks in subtlety. Clearly this is on the level of a last resort measure, when one is being closed in on. This desperate measure is used when a Ninja is being surrounded, but the pursuers are still a ways off. Fortunately, there is a temple nearby and within we spy a bell-tower, a low slung belfry or maybe a *Hanshō*[2] fire bell on an exposed veranda will catch your eye. At this point the Ninja who has exhaustively trained all of the 『Roku-Mu Shi-U』 Waza seizes the opportunity to bang the hanging bell with a Gon! or ring the *Hanshō* with a *Jya-n*! The way in which it will echo out across the lonely night is unimaginable. Reacting with a Hah! as if just knocked awake, the enemy forces will as one forget their main objective. *If they doubt they will suspect, if they become flustered and exited they will begin to move about.*

Above all they will proceed to where the hanging bell is reverberating or to where the *Hanshō* rang out from. Whether due to suspicion or out of duty they will be drawn in. This unavoidable outcome will flummox the _{calculations} intentions of the noose attempting to close tight about our neck and the strategy crumbles apart. And this from the perspective of the Ninja represents a complete breakdown f the organization of the entire enemy force. Fating hold of the chance to crush the enemy's inertia and, without the slightest gap, leveraging that seam to open a path the Ninja leaps away soundlessly into the waiting darkness like a swift nocturnal bird. Even as the echoes of the *Go-n!* or the *Jya-n!* drift out

---

[1] 割符 A medieval Japanese coat-check kind of pass. Half of a piece of paper or wood with writing on it was given and items were held until someone bearing the matching half returns. Used as security checks and later to allow ships to dock at harbors.

[2] 半鐘 A smaller verison of the big inverted-cup shaped temple bells.

『*Mabataki no Ma*』 has been used to speed out of the range of this sound. As the enemy beings eagerly searching around it becomes apparent that this has more than a whiff of Ninja to it and the search soon proves to be fruitless.

This is the 『*Kyo-Jitsu-Ten-Kan*』 switch between Truth and Lie which I have referred to frequently. While this all has to do with the 『Use of sound』 within 『*Kon Ton*』 it is simply one example presented for your consideration. 『Use of light』 when compared with say the way in which the Katana at your hip is leveraged, is much like the sensing the aroma of a single white plum blossom some distance away, while the one in front of us is actually an apricot flower made of paper.

There are still things attached to 『*Kon Ton no Jutsu*』 that remain. Probably I have had the chance to relay this more than once but:

- There was a playful-trickster Sennin named Saji who lived in ancient China.
- Once again 『*Onshin Ton Kei*』 is based on the 『*Moku-Ka-Do-Kon-Sui*』 of the *Go Gyo*.
- All the varieties of 『*Onshin Ton Kei*』 brought out and detailed up to this point must now must be taken in a mass and stuffed firmly into the 『*Go Ton.*』
- Intense learning was done under extreme conditions.
- Numerous and varied methods to overcome impossible situations were formulated.

Here, while obvious things like activating the 『Sound』 of 『*Kon Ton*』 by ringing the main bell at a Buddhist temple or the smaller *Hanshō*, things in a Shrine like a *Taiko* drum can be used along the same lines. While at first we may fret that this seems to be the odd man out as it were, we find, at the end, a way that both a horsehide or cow leather covered *Taiko* along with a cast bronze bell are to be found side by side under 『*Kon Ton.*』 The adaptability of this is something we all must ponder. As it turns out a *Taiko* at a Buddhist temple is another such thing[1]

---

[1] There is a saying in Japanese that may shed a little more light on the bell and drum conversation. 太鼓は物事の始まり、鐘は終わり *Taiko wa Monogoto no Hajimari, Kane wa Owari*. The Taiko signals the beginning of something, the bell the end.

水遁の術　（水に依って姿を消す）

Sui Ton no Jutsu　　The Art of Water Escapes

(Using Water in Order to Erase One's Form)

Water and fire are set on opposite ends of the spectrum. Having looked at 『*Ka Ton*』within the 『*Go Ton*』of Ninjutsu and its effects to a great extent we finally turn our attention to 『*Sui Ton no Jutsu*』as it takes the stage. This 『*Sui Ton*』also takes on aspects differing from the others and these are separated into the somewhat surprisingly simple categories of:

◎ 水の體を利用する場合 *Mizu no Tai wo Riyō Suru Ba-ai*
Situations Where the Body of Water is Utilized

◎ 水の性を利用する場合 *Mizu no Sei wo Riyō Suru Ba-ai*
Situations Where the Nature of Water is Utilized

◎ 水の力を利用する場合 *Mizu no Chikara wo Riyō Suru Ba-ai*
Situations Where the Power of Water is Utilized

Each of these categories, when actually done in the field, are rather surprisingly intricate. Further, as these techniques can be extremely effective 『*Sui Ton*』strains to give no ground to the powerful 『*Ka Ton*』. First of all we have to define what exactly is meant by 『Situations Where the Body of Water is Utilized.』 This concerns responding to the particular depth of the depression in the ground, how deep it may be or how wide it may be. These two together are referred to as 『The Body of the Water,』 and it is utilized according to our needs. Note that this is the typical way in which 『*Sui Ton no Jutsu*』is employed in the field by Ninja whose forte can be said to be in 『*Sui Ton*』.

In the second one of the enemy is set to sound the alarm with a half formed *Ya...!*, in that 『*Mabataku no Ma*』after an attack has been formulated but before it is engaged, we rapidly seek deep water and plunge ourselves in with a *Dopuri*! sound. Dividing the ways in which people can throw themselves into the water we end up with the following four:

◎　ザブンと飛び込む（多角式）Fly In With a *Zabun*!
　　　　　　(Multi-sided)
◎　ドプンと跳ぶ込む（少角式）Jump In With a *Dopun*!
　　　　　　(Few-sided)
◎　ドプリと落ち込む（歪圓式）Drop In With a *Dopuri*!
　　　　　　(Distorted Sphere)
◎　トプリと落ち込む（眞圓式）Fly In With a *Topuri*!
　　　　　　(Truly Spherical)

Zabun! is the least well formed of all, with the head, hands, body and feet not stowed away but in a wild shapeless mess. With your wings flapping about as you go we have no choice but to term this flying into the water. Due to all the parts sticking out we label this multi-sided as well. There is absolutely nothing becoming about smacking the water with this reverberating *Zabun*! sound. We are forced to call this reverberation something of a blowback. A *Bachyan*! splash comes right after the *Zabun*! entry.

The gist of the next one *Dobun*! is that the limbs are not flailing about nearly so much, therefore the water is only somewhat blown back and we somewhat enter the water instead of slapping on top. The flapping from before is nearly non-existent and the limbs are more fettered away. Overall somewhat more in the manner of one accustomed to the water. In this situation we call it a jump while at the same time the multi-faceted, becomes semi-faceted.

For the one in third place we remove the 『ン』 or "Nn" sound that reverberated and in place of it simply add a 『リ』 or "Ri" to give us a smooth vertical entry. Not flying in and not jumping in but rather a natural fall into the water. The angles have nearly disappeared here, and though a slight curve to the body is present it is still a gentle one, therefore we term it "Distorted Sphere."

The gist of the fourth one in line is from the start and unreserved *Topuri*! merge into the water with a smooth and quiet *Sorori*! sound. More so than the body "falling naturally" into the water this makes a purposeful, almost artistic use of the body as you slip into the water. It therefore requires a higher level of skill. Entering a the water in a kind of gentle merge is the meaning of this 『Truly Spherical[1].』

Well then, what of it? Surprising that a researcher of Ninjutsu has to be this precise and cover such a range of details? This is by no means a run-of-the-mill subject. Not at all, in fact, the Ninja have thrown themselves into the depths of 『*Sui Ton*』 with a Topuri! Those same depths we have barely begun to scratch.

Be that as it may the enemy are not like to give up easily.

"What are you going to do now then?!"

They blubber as they laugh through their noses. The laughter trails off as time stretches out so that stillness seems to have lasted a hundred years. They silently pour their full concentration on to the surface of the body of water. In the time scale we use today, ten minutes pass. Twenty minutes pass. Thirty minutes pass...no forty or maybe even fifty minutes pass. They are even becoming worn out from waiting for more or less an hour, while the Ninja is still as if asleep on the bottom of the lake or whatever and does not seem to have any intention of surfacing. Such is the length of time submerged as they will be tempted to think it was everything from a *Kawa-uso* "River Lie" or river otter to a seal or a hippo[2].

"That one's a monster of some sort, somehow he turned into a fish, we're sure to be consumed by the beast."

Utterly astounding. Fear inspiring.

The reality is hardly as frightening. Ninja have, from long in the past, developed a mechanism to deal with this. Beforehand a thin, bamboo tube some two Shaku in length is prepared. This bamboo "pipe stem" can now act like a chimney. The one you prepare should be of a thickness appropriate to grip easily. Entering the water with a *Dopuri*! sound we rapidly close off the nose. Now fully underwater we move our body slowly and deliberately along the bottom a distance of some five or six *Ken*, somewhat removing ourselves from our point of entry. We put the end of the chimney we spoke of before in our mouth. The other end

---

[1] The Kanji Itoh Sensei uses refer to something round or "spherical" but the meaning he seems to be reaching for is something along the lines of "mellow" or "gentle."

[2] 川獺　Japanese river otter.

we stick up from the surface of the water one or two *Sun*[1] and respiration can be done unhindered.

Clearly this is not something that can be done by your average person. Due to the time spent in the water training, strengthening and enduring long periods submerged, the breath can flow easily. The effect of the *Shūgyō* done in Ninjutsu, far beyond what average people are prepared to do, can be seen in the length of time they can *Gaman* this[2]. Ensuring that the end of the bamboo tube is not visible even at night is essential. Positioning ourselves amongst other floating grasses or vegetation is an obvious solution to this.

Next we have 『Situations Where the Nature of Water is Utilized.』 "Water seeks its own level" it is said and as an example, if the edge surrounding a body of water were to be broken then the water will, according to its nature, gush and flow out that point. Ninja see this as the use of the 『Power of Water.』 This is the freedom of movement possessed by water—this means in other words no matter how extended it becomes or how freely it moves about it must be dealt with as a single entity.

◎ Violently kicking water in the face of an opponent
◎ Spraying a mouth-full of water at the face of your opponent

These two represent the primary situations where the Ninja use the 『Nature of water』 for their needs. Whether being attacked by the enemy or having pursuers close on our heels, if there is water nearby then we fly towards it. Without a moment's thought we act like a caterpillar becoming a moth we change tactics as we molt and charge for water. Whether it is a pond, a river, a moat or even a drainage ditch. Even a riverbank abutting a rapid, whisking by with a *Su-re su-re*! sound. It appears to those watching that one of our legs has extended to nearly two Shaku in length and it seems as well to be acting as a ladle. Faster than the eye can follow and just at the moment they think,

"He's scooping water up!"

The face and eyes take the brunt of it. With a powerful *Sah*! the blast of

---

[1] 間　*Ken*　1.8 meters.　寸 *Sun*　3cm.
[2] 我慢 Endure. Suck it up.

water is launched and it splatters eliciting a *Gyafun*! and *Uwa*! from the enemy who opens their mouth and closes their eyes in reaction. In that interval we employ the 『*Kimari Te*』 of 『*Mabataku Ma*』 and complete our escape *Shubi yoku*[1].

This is but one of the two described above. The other one will now be outlined using the same situation and operating in the same fashion. The difference being, this time instead of the feet moving in a rapid *Haya-waza*[2] technique it is the mouth which will be the focus of our application. To our opponent's surprised eyes we are suddenly prone on the ground, at the same time the Ninja extend their neck and it seems to stretch out like a *Rokuro-kubi*[3]. We appear then as a giant snake, peering into the water from the edge. Here we wait. Then as if the very water itself were rising up, both of these techniques are put into operation in one movement. Even faster than the kick of water is the arrow projected with all our force, flying from our mouth like a *Mizu teppo*[4]. This is neither *Gya-fun* nor is it *Uwaa*, rather it is the breath getting choked off with a *Guh, Puh, Gyu*. It is said that in some situations the opponent goes tumbling head over heels.

The 『Situations Where the Power of Water is Utilized.』 There is a spectacular example of a Ninja using this. And I know, saying things like "Once upon a time, a certain Ninja...." is going to cause some to suspect this is some kind of make believe. However a fantasy tale with Saizo Kirigakure or Sasuke Sarutobi and the like it is not[5]. This is a real and

---

[1] 首尾よく Completing something fully, from Neck (head) to tail.

[2] 早業 Early (quick) + technique. Also implies skillful.

[3]  轆轤首 A female demon with a long neck. From the awesomely named Spirit and Monster Illustration Database. 怪異・妖怪画像データベース.

[4] 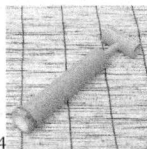 水鉄砲 "Water Musket." A piece of bamboo with a bamboo plunger. When pushed in the plunger forces the water out a small hole in the bottom.

[5] 霧隠才蔵 Saizo Kirigakure and 猿飛佐助 Sasuke Sarutobi are

true story of a real and true Ninja.

While who this is and what they may have done is likely wholly unfamiliar to the world at large, the fact of the matter is that this tale contains the particular "Aji" that is associated only with the distinct realm of Ninjutsu.

So then, a certain Ninja was tasked with an extremely important mission. As it turns out the Ninja's presence had been detected. Further amongst the enemy the five finest warriors, who were determined to prevent the Ninja's escape, were even now hard on his trail. In an impossible situation the Ninja slipped down an almost painfully narrow alley. With a riled up enemy now blocking the entrance...*Nan mu san*! The realization comes that it is a dead end[1]. Forming up across the width of the alley, the enemy readies themselves and begins to advance bristling with tension with a *Jiri-jiri* sound. To the left and right was

---

characters from a legendary group of Ninja that assisted the Samurai 眞田幸村 Sanada Yukimura during the Warring States Era. Starting in the Edo period the books were titled 真田三代記 *Sanada Sandaik*i but later became known as the 真田十勇士 *Sanada Jūyūshi* highlighting the exploits of the Ninja.

[1] 南無三 Short for 南無三宝 *Nan mu san pō*. Which is literally "The Three Treasures of The Buddah!" but is basically "Oh, my Buddah!" an exclamation when one is in need of help, has made an error, dropped a dish or whatever. And FYI the Three Treasures are:

Buddha

Referring to the historical Buddha (Siddharta) or the Buddha nature — the ideal or highest spiritual potential that exists within all beings;

Dharma

The teachings of the Buddha, the path to Enlightenment.

Sangha

The community of those who have attained enlightenment, who may help a practicing Buddhist to do the same. Also used more broadly to refer to the community of practicing Buddhists, or the community of Buddhist monks and nuns. Wikipedia.

naught but the blank walls of *Dozō* storehouses. There was only a low but securely shut up house placed at the end of the alley. At the other end was the closed off ^{chained} entrance to the alley. Well, this is it. The hands of the pursuers were nearly brushing the Ninja's back.

At this point the Ninja suddenly fixed his eye on a *Mizu-game*[1] so large it seemed like to reach the porch eves. In all likelihood it was used as a receptacle to call the water from the heavens down off the roof. In the moment the warriors come racing up from behind, like a human avalanche, in that second, the Ninja moves. Leaping in a great near inhuman jump he tucks his legs under and flies some six or seven Shaku through the air, landing in the *Mizu-game* with a *Zubori*! splash. Instantly the *Mizu-game* splintered and scattered with a *Bara-bara*! sound. However many Koku of water were held in that *Mizu-game* all came exploding out like a giant ocean wave striking a rock and turning to snow. The force is as if a giant bomb erupted. To the left and right the featureless *Dozō* storehouses, the alley itself is rather narrow to begin with and we get, almost as a bonus the imposing front wall of the house at the end of the street. The enemy, now blasted with water complains to it fruitlessly *"Why is it only us who is being pelted with these fragments of water jar?"* A water bomb. With dangerous things mixed in. They are hit in the head, bathed in water and collapse in a disorganized jumble with an Ah! When they finally come around the Ninja is long gone.

This is, in no uncertain terms, a classic example of the use of 「The Power of Water」 for our 『*Kimari no Te*.』 Should one violently rouse the water which has sat serenely for such a long time, the anger that erupts ill surpass even the burn of fire. Clearly to the greatest extent of its ability, water conceals its power. Cutting open an embankment or smashing a dike will cause no small amount of damage, therefore if done, our crime is like to be dealt with strictly by our superiors. Thus the use of the 「Power of Water」 of 『Sui Ton』 is restricted for use by Ninja to situations where people will not be made to suffer.

---

[1] 水甕 An earthenware water "barrel" usually about waist to chest high.

水道の術者が大水
甕に躍り込み數石
の水と甕の破片と
を爆發するが如く
飛び散らして追手
たる五名の勇士を
驚き倒れさせる圖

An illustration of a person using *Sui Ton no Jutsu*. He leaps into a *Mizu-game* causing several *Koku* of water as well as shards of *Mizu-game* to explode out. The five brave warriors are so stunned by this that they are toppled.

裏の五遁は略説に止める

The Ura Goton will only be Covered in Outline Form

As I have already formally introduced and explained each element of the 『*Onshin Ton Kei,*』 properly defined as the *Moku-Ka-Do-Kon-Sui* set which is patterned after the 『Go Gyo』 my brush has expanded deeply into the *Gokui* "mysterious" secrets. In addition to the above 『Omote』 or "Obverse" we have the 『Ura』 or "Reverse" and the five varieties *Nin-Kin-Jyu-Chu-Gyo* that make up this Goton. For this section as well I intend to lay out just the basic framework of it to my readers.

Now, and somewhat by chance, the time to explain The Ura Goton has arrived. Just before I get into that, it needs to be stated that there is no d i f f e r e n c e [distance or seperation] between the entirety of Goton that flows through the 『*Kimari Te*』 and that which flows through the 『*Oku no Te*』 of the 『*Onshin Tonkei.*』 And that is not the whole of it. From the beginning if you understand the Omote or "obverse" of something, the Ura or "reverse" does not extend beyond the end of where that thing ends is. It can be said then that if you understand this, you, yourself can understand that as well. If you achieve understanding of one side it follows quite reasonably that the other side will be absorbed as well.

Due to these circumstances, and in order to avoid having both the author and reader running around in circles, I have explained the Ura Go Ton only in outline fashion. I will only elucidate on such portions that pertain to 『*Mabataku Ma no Hataraki.*』 In addition to the names of each, the meanings, but moreover the particularities and uses of the unusual items carried and other such points, will be touched on.

The above-mentioned are, just to be sure, the following five:

人遁 Jin Ton　　Human Escapes

禽遁 Kin Ton　Bird Escapes

獣遁 Jyu Ton　Beast Escapes

蟲遁 Chu Ton Insect/Small Creature Escapes

魚遁 Gyo Ton Fish Escapes

The one placed in the first position is Jin Ton no Jutsu. While this involves using people to conceal oneself, as is written in the Hikan "Secret Scroll" Nindo *Ware wo motte Ta to Nashi, Ta wo motte Ware to Nasu* suddenly borrowing and making use of a person's body other than your own, without remorse, in order to conceal your own form. In other words this is none other than the Ninja technical term for 『*Kyo-Jitsu Ten Kan*』, namely the operation which is the 『*Mabataku no Ma.*』

The second is Kin Ton. As before this mainly focuses on working with birds, primarily chickens, ducks, geese and so on. In the daytime they are typically gathered in flocks around peoples' houses while at night such birds are gathered in one part of the house or a nest attached to it. Yard birds are extremely easy to startle and moreover, once startled can be easily made to run amok with shrill shrieks, calls, flapping about and other mayhem which, upon occasion we can make use of. In this case it is not 『*Kyo-Jitsu Ten Kan*』 but rather should be referred to using the language 『*Chu-i Ten Kan.*』 In addition、 of course nested birds like crows and the like can be made use of, though as their roosts tend to be high up in trees additional costly time must be spent therefore the efficacy is difficult to judge.

Third is *Jū* Ton. This operates much like the Jin Ton which is in the first position, namely carrying out the 『*Kyo-Jitsu Ten Kan*』 of 『*Ta wo Mote, Ware to Nasu.*』 Concealing yourself behind the nose and face of a cow emerging from the gloom of night, or, in the jumble things become in the early evening, moving in on the flank of a pack horse and, using it in place of yourself, grabbing up its reins and directing it right at the noses of one's pursuers.

Of course at the same time we also have situations that use 『*Mabataku Ma no Hataraki.*』 A rat or two that have gotten used to you after being captured with a bit of glue made of *Konyaku*[1] and carried about in a jute[2] pouch on the waist. Upon the occasion one is slipping

---

[1] 蒟蒻糊 Konyaku Jelly Paste. From a plant of the same name used to make a kind of gelatin used in Oden and Sukiyaki as well as snacks

[2] 麻囊 Asabukuro. A pouch made of the Jutte plant which can be spun

into a castle or palace the rat can be released and an effective application of the technique of 『*Chu-i Ten Kan*』 will affect the *bushi*^samurai guardsmen. This is more or less the "formal" way *Jū* Ton is carried out. This, in other words is *Nezumi* "Rat" Jutsu. In addition to this, fresh fruit from the *Matatabi*[1] plant or a pinch of the salted, preserved version could be tossed into a fireplace calling all the cats in half a *Cho*[2] to the area. This will have everyone up in arms in surprise allowing for a 『*Chu-i Ten Kan*.』 Truth be told the kind of *Matatabi* that you can purchase from a chemist has only a limited effect. The fruit is the best. On another note a hemp bag can be coated with *Konyaku* glue and, if hung out in the shade is unlikely to be gnawed at by rats.

The fourth one to arrive is Chu Ton "Insect/small creature Escapes". The "formal" use of this is, as you may have guessed, like that with the rat, namely carrying about a pet snake or toad and in the same manner utilize it. In other words we have *Hebi* "Snake" no Jutsu lined up with *Gama* "Toad" no Jutsu. When speaking of Hebi, the *Aodaisho*[3] or Japanese Rat Snake comes to mind, its appearance and markings serve as its "armour". Fully extended it is around three or four *Shaku*[4] in length and fairly docile, therefore it can be wrapped up in a bit of nice writing paper or even some course *Nishi no uchi*[5] paper and carry it like a package of *Daifuku* pounded rice cakes with bean jelly in one's breast pocket.

When speaking of Gama, the *Hikigaeru*[6] ones are the biggest ones. If you make your way into dark damp valleys you can captures specimens like this alive. In the city of Susono near Mt. Fuji the author himself discovered a toad the size of an iron kettle, while amongst the mountains

---

into coarse, strong threads. Among vegetable fibers Jute is second only to cotton in amount produced and variety of uses.

[1] 木天蓼 Also known as Silver Vine has long been known to elicit euphoric response in cats. The reaction to *Matatabi* is similar to the catnip response, but appears to be more intense. Long a traditional medicine in Asia for its relief of arthritic pain relief possible cancer treatments are being investigated.

[2] 町 A unit of measure about 110 meters.

[3] 青大将 Blue+big+leader. A non-venomous snake found all over Japan.

[4] 尺 One *shaku* is about 30 centimeters.

[5] 西の内紙 A cheap, course but tough paper.

[6] 蟇蛙 Common Japanese toad.

of Akita, I found one the bigger than three adult heads put together. These things are incredibly mild mannered and can be put into a cloth sack and carried on the waist as one walks around easier than one can carry ones lunch. As with the *Nezumi*, the *Hebi* gliding along and the *Gama* plodding along will draw attention in the same way and how that interval can be used should be examined. In the case where "Futari no Nin" is being used, the first person will make their way to where the mistress of the house spends her time, or other place where only women are likely to be gathered. The obvious effect of using this *Hebi* or *Gama* is that screams of *Gyaaa!, Hiiii, What is that!* and so one are going to cause this women's world to go amok. This uproar is going to extend into the man's world of the palace and night watch and its *Bushi* (Samurai) are going to come with swords drawn to find the source of the ruckus. The way it works is that in the ensuing confusion, the second person can complete the task.

There are some additional points I would like to add. If a person were to scurry along the rafters like a Nezumi, or make as a toad on the ground immobile as a stone, or slip beneath the floor and move as if without breath, in addition slither like a snake through narrow paths or move without sound are all variations of *Nezumi no Jutsu, Gama no Jutsu* and *Hebi no Jutsu.*

As for the fifth one in line Gyo Ton "Fish Escapes", it's frankly impossible. One can of course do the same as with the chickens and ducks and surprise the Koi in the pond into splish-splashing about and then use that 『*Chu-i Ten Kan*』 for your 『*Shunkan Sayo*』 and it would become Gyo Ton no Jutsu. But this seems to be stretching things a bit toward improbability. It seems like the whole situation could be handled better with Sui Ton no Jutsu. The whole issue lies with the *shape* format many people from long ago learned and were bound to. The ninja that came out of this were fixated on the fact that 『*Onshin Ton Kei*』 contained an 『*Omote Go Ton*』 and that this was matched by an 『*Ura Go Ton.*』 Due to this there was no choice other than to pull up the fish and draw up a seat up at the table for the possibly redundant *Sakana*. All in all there are many points that don't sit right in the minds of modern people today. This is nothing but the difference that comes with a changing of era. The above passage stands in testament to that very fact.

This is where I could put to rest the rhythm *Goton! Goton!* of *Juton!*, but not for the element of the flexibility of 『Go Ton no Jutsu』 that remains unexplained. This is defined as either 『一遁単用 *Itton Tan You* Using a single Ton Technique Alone』 or 『数遁供用 *Su Ton Kyo Yoh* Multiple Ton Applied in Unison.』 For example if Ka Ton is to be used then Ka Ton it is, but if one decides to make use of the remaining four Ton, then one or two, three or four or all of them can be utilized as an amalgam.

Well there is remains much to be covered with this topic, however the point of this chapter was to elucidate on the Ninjutsu of yore, so I will restrain my brush at this point. The point that should be the most surprising is how the Ninja of long ago managed to successfully train until their minds and body were as one, this spectacular achievement that one can almost define as beyond that of normal humans. Even beyond this is the fact that the Shūgyō is a violent, intense, amazing and frightful thing, something that seemingly cannot, cannot be done by mortal flesh and bone. It simply astonishes and takes the breath away to the point one can hardly recall what one has seen.

In the end people of today have bundled all of this up to certain degree as nothing more than a pack of lies, slapstick or outright bullshit. Be that as it may, proof trumps theory. Right now we have the Fourteenth Inheritor of the Kouga Ryu Isamushi Fujita also known by his 武号 *Bugo* martial arts name Seiko. That this single legitimate successor of the teachings of Ninjutsu exists today is truly a marvel. This person is able to absolutely flabbergast academics, experts and any other person of status with his mysterious feats of physicality. They simply cannot comprehend the path of training that the Ninja had to travel down. Those that are not Ninja but rather ordinary citizens-namely my collected readers should understand that the author is, by himself attempting to delve into the topic of what Ninjutsu is and would not relay anything not rooted in fact.

Even should someone attempt to imitate Mr. Fujita, there is not really anything to worry about as people these days do not have the knowhow necessary to endure the difficult, painful, turbulent, extreme, startling and frightening path. To be frank, even should people of today give up their *Keiko* or *Shūgyō*-in other words abandon their studies or craft-there really is no need for them to endure the hellish absorption of these techniques to their bodies. This book is crafted to pull from that art that has no parallels in the past or present-that which only Ninjutsu has been able to develop and forge in strict discipline—the 『Shunkan Sayo』 in other words The Function of the Eye Blinking. The goal is basically to fit perfectly together this 『Gendai-teki Goshin Jutsu,』 defined as the most effective method for protecting oneself, along with 『Gendai-teki Syosei Jutsu,』 in other words the most effective way to make ones way in the world. Taking from the Shūgyō of the Ninja of the past just what is needed for oneself in this modern world is what should be done. Now, at long last let's do just that.

其の四

忍術の現代的練習法はこれだ

Chapter Four

This is the Modern Ninjutsu Training Regimen

At last we have come to explain the methods for learning and the methods for strengthening. That being said tedious explanations and long sections on theory will be for the most part abbreviated and consideration has been taken so that the *Kaname*[1] or vital points are clearly and succinctly delineated. With this intention in mind I would like to ask for my readers' attention as I discuss this stage.

Before anything else we must delve into the most effective method of protecting oneself in these times, namely that which is based on the Ninjutsu *Shūgyō*. We begin by gathering the four foundation elements and introducing them. They are the following four.

◎ A strong body (A strong and vigorous b o d y) [frame]
◎ Nimble responses (Having light and quick movement)
◎ A finely tuned mind (A detailed and accurate head) [brain]
◎ Having mental acumen (A sharp discerning working of the spirit)

Clearly one who has all four of these traits from the outset is exceptional. If this is not the case and your body is somewhat on the weak side or your reactions are on the slow side or your brain is prone to daydreaming or [head] should your spirit be somewhat insensitive then work to knead that one of the four until it becomes harder. Develop that ability, moreover by doing so, should a chance present itself that ability will immediately begin to rush out in a torrent. When you are going or stopping, sitting or laying down throughout the year, without exception keep your head alert [sleeping] and build up *Tanren*[2] in your spirit. Building layer upon layer by using

---

[1] 要 The vital points, essence.
[2] 鍛錬 Discipline, forging the spirit.

your *Ki*[1] in the process of your continuing Shūgyō, and at any and all points during this looking back and considering your b o d y ^{frame} its core and operation, your brain ^{head} and its core and working. The point must be reached whereupon *the four* are all working together and intertwined. At the same time we also have:

◎ 能力の養成（能力を養ふこと）

The Developing ones Abilities (The cultivation of one's abilities ^{power})

◎能力の行使（能力を使ふこと）

The Exercising of ones Abilities (The using of one's abilities ^{power})

    These are as people are wont to like: killing two birds with one stone. Normally people are out at the edge trying to reach towards the *Moto* or ideal structure, imagine then, if you will, a person who from the outset is at this *Moto*-in other words has a b o d y ^{frame} and a brain ^{head} already equipped with the four foundations. That person would not have to start from the edge and work inward by developing their abilities ^{strength} and using their abilities ^{power} but rather simply release their spirit according to their will.

    Thus we end this chapter on those whose line of work was that of a Ninja. We can take their same difficult, severe, violent and hard "foundation building" and create a method whereupon we can snap-it-up right quickly. Once we have done our "foundation building" the next thing we have is, at last, the thing that is incomparable now or in the past, that which shines out only from the golden star of the Ninjutsu of Japan-which if we refer to as was done in the past we get 『*Mabataku Ma no Hataraki* Moving in the interval of the operation of the eye』 or the 『*Mabataki no Hataraki Operation during the working of the eye*』 - which if we use modern language we arrive at the *Shūgyō* of 『Shunkan Sayo.』

---

[1] 気 Fighting spirit.

◎ 第一には察眼の練習 　The First is Training in Developing an Observant Eye.

This is when someone is walking towards you, or when you are in a building or inside a room and someone comes up beside you. Take a

head on

glance at their eyes and should there be something to the light in them or the color. Something small or some kind of shift that means that that person means to attack, intimidate or otherwise make use of you. This 『Ki no Ugoki』 should be quickly observed and distinguished as part of your training.

peek

◎ 第二には挫気の練習 　The Second is Training in Breaking the *Ki*.

Through observation you can detect by the position of the opponent's eye whether they are attempting to attack you or intimidate you with 『*Ki no Ugoki.*』 Next we must determine when the opponent has truly determined to attack, but in the moment before release. Imagine then an even a closer shave and he is *already engaging.* That very 『*Mabataku no Ma* 』 moment must be captured with the *Guu!*—sound of a gripping fist. That 『*Shunkan,*』 that chance must be snatched up, neither too early nor too late, like a single strand of hair. Reacting like a whisk of wind you move, beating your opponent to the punch, cracking open the front of his attack and effectively breaking his head of steam-all the while lightly, nimbly, finely, discerningly-this is Shūgyō in operating like a flash of lightning.

◎ 第三には隠身の練習
The third is training in *Onshin*, or concealing the body.

So through the *Shunkan* split second operation the head of steam was forestalled, the front of his attack was broken and through his *Ki* being broken the body also falls apart. If this collapse can be drawn forth, then, without delay, rapidly remove yourself to a place outside the field of vision of the opponent all the while operating with the same lightning speed. Ideally, this would be a place beyond the physical reach of the opponent, namely a safe spot where 　one could preserve oneself and make an escape-this sort of *Shūgyō*.

Once having thoroughly gone through and moved past this his three-layered *Shūgyō*, or in other words reached the point where the principals of Ninjutsu are met, namely 「Neither inflicting injury upon him, nor allowing injury to befall yourself, this and only this is *Jyō-Nin¹.*」 And this is itself the *Shūgyō* method for 「*Gendai-Teki Goshin Jutsu*」.

For this to be practically applicable, the three principles thoroughly laid out in the chapter titled 『Where do the strengths and possibilities for victory lie in Ninjutsu?』 are necessary. As described the triptych of 『The situation whereupon one uses their own implements』, 『The situation whereupon one uses implements not your own』 and 『The situation whereupon one uses your own implements as well as implements not your own』 come into play in the second after the opponent's *Ki* has been broken and the "nose" of his attack crushed.

There are of course a variety of implements that can be utilized, however for day-to-day Shūgyō there is already a method. First find a training partner or *Aite²*. Taking turns, establish who will be the attacker and who the defender and go full out. In order to acquire acquiring the 『*Mabataku Ma no Hataraki*』 an open hand should fly like a bolt of lightning, moving across the eyes at a distance of two or three *Sun³*. This is appropriate Keiko for when using items while the open hand strike itself can be made use of in real situations as well.

That being said, in reality two to three Sun is still a bit weak. Really the attack should reach to the eyebrows, but as this is somewhat dangerous for *Keiko*, it serves to stop a little short. To make up for this, the strike across the eyes with the hand should be of sufficient speed as to make a sound when cutting through the air. The resulting gust of wind should be such that it blows air into the eyes⁴.

At the same time and working in tandem with the hand, the feet should be moving quickly, moreover accurately. Coupled together with this are the hips, which should be placed effectively and moreover move smoothly and lightly. That all these elements are unified is a

---

1 彼を傷つけず己れも傷つかずして危きを凌ぐは忍の上になるもの
KarewoKizu tsukezuOnoremoKizutsukazu shi teAyauKi woShinoguwaNinnoJyoninarumono

2 相手 Training partner who takes the role of adversary.
3 寸 One sun is equivalent to 3.03 cm.
4 Itoh Sensei describes this attack as a 払う *harau* or sweeping motion.

fundamental element of *Shūgyō*.

If fashioned into a chart showing order, it would look something like this:

（表）手—足—腰

Omote or obverse------Hand------Feet-----Hips

（裏）腰—足—手

Ura or reverse----------Hips-------Feet-----Hand

The Omote has the hand as the priority while assisting that the feet are in second position. Helping the feet are the hips, which of course are therefore in third position. If we switch around and look at the Ura, we find that we have the exact opposite. Should the hips not be placed effectively, the feet will be late to move. If the feet are delayed then the hand will not reach its target and thus a chance to manipulate the interval of a blink of an eye will be lost. Further the core of the body will flounder and there is the fear you may put yourself in harm's way. Therefore and thusely the ordering of and function of each element within the Omote and Ura should not be ignored. It is of essence that Keiko should include both elements as one whole.

The next second, which has, up until now been waiting arrives without the slightest pause onto the stage to take the center spot. The hand has finished its task and completely turns control over to the hips. They move precisely and without the slightest loss of time while the feet take their cue from the placement of the hips. It should be noted that this lightning like speed coupled with an unflustered, certain manner of leaping in is fundamental.

The thrust of this is that whether you are guarding your country or protecting yourself, there is only one underlying principal. This thing called aggressive defense is, in this day and time, considered relevant irrespective of the country. And necessary no matter what the people. And therefore this method for defending against attack, namely the Ninjutsu technique of 『Shunkan Sayo』 used within the framework of 『Gendai-teki Goshin Jutsu』 is also therefore duly established as relevant. The caveat to this is that *one needs an objective to accomplish* for this Ninjutsu. In the past using techniques in a trifling manner or otherwise mucking about was said to be strictly prohibited. The entirety of the applications of Ninjutsu were meant to protect one's body. Should a person these days veer from the path of 『Goshin Jutsu』 and attempt to cleverly apply this for profit, it would be the case of a little learning being a terrible thing.

The "reward" would be instantly dropping off and away from the 『Nin no Michi』 and thusly things would go topsy-turvy and the body would likely be injured if not destroyed in my view. Here prudence is required.

If we move another step forward, we have that which is a step beyond 『Goshin Jutsu』 the 『Gendai-teki Shosei Jutsu』. In other words (and as I have exhaustively detailed before) I am referring to the Ninjutsu Shūgyō, which should be considered as the most effective, all-encompassing technique. What if we were to take the 『Shun Kan Sayo』 and in place of striking out with the body were instead to replace it with striking out strategically with the will? This would be the result of developing layer upon layer of *Kufū*[1] and, moreover, compiling a resume of practicing it in the field. In other words, should a decision present itself, or when starting some sort of consultation, or perhaps a person comes to consult or discuss something with you and you are subject to a wave of intimidating language. In this and other situations one can be like "let it come then!" and gladly accept it. One will be able to perceive the way you can maintain an advantageous position, ride the blink of an eye chance to activate your spirit and quickly deflect the opponent's *Ki*. His *Hokosaki*[2] or spear point deflected, one can move in again and one will become able to cause the *Aite* to deviate left or right according to ones will. Moving from a normal manner to a state of having intent is an interesting feeling I believe. For those two concentrated seconds, the reason for Shūgyō in focused release of the sprit becomes clear.

We will revisit another aspect of this topic at another point, but for now that ends the Shūgyō method for that thing applicable the world over, Ninjutsu.

---

[1] 工夫 Techniques or "little tricks" one develops to get around obstacles.
[2] 鋒 Point of a spear. Point of an attack.

第一圖

對手の目の中にそ
の氣の動きを察し
て、隙かさや先手
を打つべく、此方
から發し掛かって
而もまだ目立たせ
ぬ形
（向つて左）

右手を開いて下げた
のは餘念がない樣に
見せて而も向ふの目
先を捕ふ仕度

右足の踵が少し上が
つてゐる所に注意せ
よ

Illustration One:

First you detect Ki no Ugoki, or something in the opponent's face. Without allowing a gap you must make the initial strike yourself first. Note that none of this is apparent. (The figure facing us on the left). The right hand is open and down and appears not ready, but it is prepared to strike at the eyes of the one across from him. You should take care to note that the heel of the right foot is slightly off the ground.

第二圖

素早く飛び込んで
對手の眉毛先を平、
手で拂つた瞬間の
形。但し第一圖の
形から右足を一歩
進め、下げた右手
は肱を曲げて胸先
まで上げ、拵ひ手
の用意をすると同
時に、兩足飛びに
腰を据ゑて飛び込
む。

點線は一歩進めた姿勢

Illustration Two:

This shows the position the body takes the second you fly in and strike across the opponent's eyebrows. Note that the right foot has proceeded one step forward from the first illustration. The elbow of the right hand, which hangs by your sided is bent up to chest level and readied. At the same time jumping in with both feet adjusting them with your hips.

The dotted line denotes the positioning during the first step.

第
三
図

平手で睫毛先を拂
はれた對手が、先
づ反り身になつた
次の瞬間に、腰砕
けとなつて體を崩
した形。その瞬間
に、此方は素早く
身を脱するので、
續けて二瞬間の利
用が眼目である。

Illustration Three:

The opponent who has been swiped across the eyes with an open
hand just at the edge of the eyebrows will have stuck his chest out.
In the next second his hips will falter and his balance will be
completely taken. From that second we rapidly remove ourselves.
Making use of this two second interval is the essential point.

其の五

Sono Go

氣分轉換と注意轉換との實効及び例證

The Practical Effects and Examples of Kibun Tenkan and Chu-i Tenkan

In a nutshell, in order to guard one's body turning to what the world is now seeing anew, the particular operation of the 『*Mabataku Ma*』 of Ninjutsu allows the techniques drilled into one's body to immediately and directly turn the intent of the *Aite,* or the opponent, around or move his attention elsewhere. This applies to the previously mentioned 『*Kibun Tenkan*』 and likewise with the following 『*Chui Tenkan.*』

If we were to break these two down simply, 『*Kibun Tenkan*』 is, basically, taking the violent technique the opponent has directed at you and striking out first, smashing the lead of his attack and in the ensuing split second of the 『*Mabataku no Ma*』 , in the second of the opponent's surprised gasp, make away. When speaking of 『*Chui Tenkan*』 one is dealing with the intent of your opponent utterly and completely crystallized on you, and at the exact moment the chip of flame from the heat of his attack comes off, rapidly and through cleverness force the operation of the Mabataku Ma. In a whisk his concentration is shifted to another place and we can take advantage of the chance that has been made available. The effect of the Shun-Kan Sayo of 『*Goshin Jutsu*』 falls into the category of either 『*Kibun Tenkan*』 or 『*Chu-i Tenkan.*』

If, for example, one were not aware of the 『*Shun Kan Sayo*』 of Ninjutsu and should you be forced to deal with some sort of extreme situation, your body would act instinctively, without your knowledge. This inborn ability to operate instinctively will activate *Waza* or technique. In less time than it takes to expel a breath this operation is completed, more frequently than one would imagine.

Further let us take a fortunate person with a strong healthy body, a light and nimble frame matched with an equally blessed precise, fine-tuned sensitive spirit. Layer atop this base an innate ability that activates to protect the body. If we add to this training in 『Goshin

Jutsu,』 worked to the level that they are well within the realm that can be called fluent then should an encounter present itself, it can, without undue trouble or fear be negotiated successfully.

Even should one not be a superb athlete or mentalist, there can be no illusion[mistake] as to the overall effect of conducting Shūgyō in striking out with the spirit.

Even by itself the 『Shosei Jutsu』 encourages a great deal of interest, matching that of the former section and I believe that there is no need to further dwell on it.

Now for the benefit of those conducting Shūgyō in 『*Gendai-teki Goshin Jutsu*』 and its parallel 『*Gendai-teki Shoshin Jutsu*』 I will present a fairly wide array of examples of rather famous historical and modern day figures whose innate ability to carry out 『Shunkan Sayo』 feature prominently.

We have the pride of Japan, he who entered the grave some three hundred years before our time and still is held in high regard, namely Hideyoshi Toyotomi[1]. As a youth in the time of crashings of great armies, at some point he joined up with Koroku Hatchisuke[2] as most of you are already aware. At the time the Koroku group was conducting itself as a band of robber-Bushi. One night the band had forced its way into a wealthy manor house out in the countryside. By chance the "little monkey"-referring to the future Hideyoshi-was, by chance, left behind. Well, this was a tight spot. A cry of "Thief! Thief!" went out and people came rushing out from eight directions, cutting off the escape routes of the "little monkey". At that moment there was a soul piercing scream emitted followed by a *Ploosh!* sound of someone having jumped into the well. "That thieving bastard jumped into the well!" they shouted and the group moving in broke up and each decided to make for the well. And there they gathered. In fact this stratagem was the result of the operation of the "little monkey's" wits. Poking his head over the lip of the well, letting out a wail and pitching in a stone he picked up somewhere along the way. In other words a perfect example of 『*Chu-i Tenkan.*』 In the

---

[1] 豊臣 秀吉 (1536 -1598) Despite rather humble beginnings he went on to bring an end to the Sengoku Era and unify the political factions of Japan.
[2] 蜂須賀小六 also known as Hachisuka Masakatsu 蜂須賀 正勝 (1526 – 1586). A military leader and eventual retainer of Toyotomi Hideyoshi .

time the mob gathered around the well the little monkey was pulling his lower eyelid down and sticking out his tongue outside the main gate[1].

A man who needs no introduction, the master swordsmith Kotestu Nagasone[2], whose style of sword making if forever associated with the Shinto of the Tokugawa era, has a surprising past. Initially he was not in fact a swordsmith but rather, if we investigate, a Gu-soku Shi[3] or, in other words and armourer. To summarize then, there was a Gu-soku Shi who went over to a famous swordsmith. "Yeah that sword there couldn't slice through my armour." The reply was equally straight "That armour could be cut clean through with my sword."

The long and the short of it is they got worked up into a bit of a boasting war in their quest to appeal for patronage. Eventually, a somewhat strange "Let's have a bout between sword and armour!" burst out and a bight with live weapons was decided upon. The Gu-soku Shi donned his own armour himself and lined himself up across from the swordsmith, set his feet and said "Come on then!" The swordsmith brought forth the sword he forged himself and raised it in Kamae[4] above his head. He came forward with such an intense influx of pure will as to surely be able to slice his sword through impenetrable castle walls. The Gu-soku Shi burst out with "Give me a moment" that sort of sucked the tension right out of the situation. The Gu-soku Shi made as if to adjust some minor part of his defenses and then said "I am ready."

The now impatient swordsmith let loose a ferocious *Ei-!* and sliced down. Was this gentleman ever surprised! The Gu-soku had only grunted and slid somewhat to one side, nothing out of the ordinary. The Katana, on the other hand, snapped clean off at just where it meets the Tsuba. In the end, of course a shout of *Kotetsu Banzai!* welled up. Even more surprising was that as the swordsmith stood frozen in his own shop the winning Gu-soku Shi disappeared without a trace. Nobody knew what the heck was going on.

Several years later, from out of thin air, the Gu-soku Shi re-appears,

---

[1] 赤目 Akame. "Red eye" Showing the red bit of your eye to ridicule someone. Itoh Sensei writes it as Akan-beh.
[2] 長曾禰 虎徹 (c. 1597–1678) Born into a family of armorers, he eventually became a famous sword smith.
[3] 具足師 An armourer.
[4] 構 A particular stance.

but this time he has transformed himself into a swordsmith. And so he sayeth:

> *I sort of pulled a fast one then. That fired blade had so much pure intent embedded in it that even the armour I made would have absolutely been like a melon split clean on its vertical. Hesitating not a moment I went to deflate him somewhat. Unbelievably in the end it was completely effective. It all came down to Ki in the end. In fact there is no method for making armour that can resist a blade, therefore I became a swordsmith instead to exceed his skill. The fact of the matter is I didn't want to be known as a sneak.*

This is the 『Kibun Tenkan』 of Kotetsu.

One day in the waning days of the Meiji Emperor[1], a cabinet meeting was being held. The Minister of Commerse, Gotō Shojiro[2] was giving an eloquent oration. As he spoke he struck those in attendance dead center. The thought amongst those present was that "This cloud is going to continue its torrential downpour until tomorrow morning!" as the voluminous speech pelted them in the face. Just then The Minister of the Navy Saigō Jūdō[3] moved as if a thought had just occurred to him, stood and walking nonchalantly over to behind the orator slid his chair some three *Shaku*[4] back from its position. The orator at this point was in the process of building to his big finish so took absolutely no notice of these actions. At long last he blasted out a flawless conclusion, took out his handkerchief to wipe the sweat from his brow and began to lower himself into his seat. He ended up thumping down on the floor in a heap. An eloquent speech rendered moot by a rather unnatural ending becomes somewhat of an ironic use of 『*Kibun Tenkan.*』

Now we are in a new era and we have a new man of talent Tōru Hoshi[5] and we find him on his way to a political summit in Niigata. In

---

[1] 明治天皇 Meiji Emperor. (1852 –1912) Ruled from 1867 until his death.
[2] 後藤 象次郎 (1838 –1897).
[3] 西郷 従道(1843 –1902) A follower of the 薬丸自顕流 Yakumaru-jigen style of sword fighting.
[4] 尺 One *Shaku* is 30.3 cm.
[5] 星享 (1850-1901) A politician.

those days political debates took on an air of a bloody battlefield. Dozens of ruffians from a rival party gathered in groups on the rooftops of buildings that lined the narrow streets. This was at a time when automobiles were something of a rarity, so Mr. Hoshi was relatively easy to spot riding in his rickshaw. A hail of fist sized stones rained down from above.

Toru then pulled out a large western - style umbrella as if it were actual raining[1] and locked his hands firmly on his knees. This was somewhat of an uncommon sight to be sure. Intriguingly the hail of rocks only seemed to bounce off the umbrella when they hit, the "bones" of it holding fast instead of cracking and splintering. From what I'm told, Hoshi was feeling a bit uneasy about the overall level of safety having been roughed up a bit in Tokyo. He went so far as to drop large sum of money on an umbrella covered with a material stiffer than crocodile hide on the occasion he had travelled to The United States. Now it is unmistakably that umbrella to which we are referring. That being said the real story starts from here. What sort of risky stunt would Hoshi attempt under that rain of small stones? Hoshi's umbrella along with Hoshi himself approached the last checkpoint. On the roofs above, seven or eight of the finest of the ruffians waited, each with one rank larger of stone, roughly as big as an Oyawan[2].   With two burly hands each lifted their rock above their heads. "Think that cursed umbrella is pretty clever? You think you can just slide on by like a wild boar without getting the full force of our might!?" Further, they poured the scorn on with

"Hunched over there like you are praying to the clouds in the sky!"

Glancing up an seeing this scene, Toru instantly stood up, collapsed his umbrella and with a shout of *Kasa! Kasa! Kasa!*[3] Stabbed the point of the umbrella right at the eyes of the ruffians. Catching them off guard they looked at each other in bewilderment and in that second, and I am not making this up, the chap simply rode his rickshaw on by.

We have to give this gentleman credit for a peculiar use of 『*Kibun*

---

[1] 蝙蝠傘 Koumori gasa. Due to their shape, resembling bat wings.
[2] 親椀 A large plain wooden bowl usually for serving soup.
[3] 傘 Umbrella! Umbrella! Umbrella!

Tenkan.』 [1]

Here is another story that I heard regarding a statesman in his prime. Despite being old and withered this leaf has not yet fallen from the branch so of course to call him by name would be out of the question. Unlike the handling of historical figures I will used different Chinese Characters to represent his name. Thus he is perhaps called Yukio Ozaki and this might have taken place in Niigata or it could have occurred in a completely different place and another city. At any rate it involves this eminent member of the Constitutional Reform Party, a rather genuine fellow.

This takes up the thread of the last tale even farther along as the man in question had already descended from the rickshaw and the end of his cane was clacking on the ground ad he walked to the entrance of the speech hall. Waiting for his chance in among the crowds of people gathered to see the famous gentlemen was none other than a member of one of those opposition parties. Leaping from the mass of spectators with a cudgel raised high, this man needed to be dealt with in short order. In that instant, faster than one can expel a breath, the defensive mechanism of our hero, his shapeless bodyguard recognized a threat and activated Mr.Ozaki's defensive instincts. In that moment Sensei was puffing on a cigarette and faster than the soul extinguishing fear that comes from the realization of danger can be felt, his hand activated of its own volition. Raising his hand with the flame tipped cigarette still gripped he stabbed forward with a rushing sound. In this situation as well the ruffian was caught out, as the flame whisked towards the eyes. Despite this "flame" being nothing more than the merest kernel, it moved with the speed of a spark cracking off a fire. This caused things to go topsy turvey for our hired thug, whose on defensive reactions were called forth. The first wave of surprise struck him and at nearly the same time linchpin in his hips came loose and with a spectacular thud he fell flat on his back. Even more surprised than the gathered spectators at this startling attack and its bewildering finish was our lecturer. The level of his astonishment can't be expressed in a tale without exiting the world of

---

[1] It turns out he was later assassinated in 1901 by the10th Heir of the Shingyo Sword School 心形刀流 a certain Iba Sotaro 伊庭 想太郎 possibly due to graft. The school was actually the sword instructors or *Shihan* 師範 for the Bakufu.

reality. An extremely rare application of 『*Kibun Tenkan,*』 isn't it?[1]

When lining up examples of this sort even breaking a whole regiment of troops into a single rank is an insufficient measure. Therefore to round things off I have decided to place an episode from the author's own youth here at the end. I humbly offer this and hope to beg your pardon for imposing it on you.

There was a festival in full swing in a small country town. I had gotten separated from my friends and was weaving through the crowd by myself. A group of boisterous fellows appeared in front of me and this cluster was none other than the local gang of troublemakers. Needless to say we were like dogs and monkeys[2]. Needless to say, despite their strength in numbers and my lack thereof, showing any sort of weakness was out of the question. There being nothing for it I made to pass by ^{rub} them. With a sudden recognition though, one twisted the bow[3] in his hands horizontally and with a challenging look blocked my passage. That first move brought the train to a full stop and the mass formed a loose oval around me. In that moment I felt something like a switch in my ^{head} brain clicking and I made as if someone had shoved me from behind. I unintentionally yank the bow away faster than I was able to register that the hands held it rather loosely. No, I didn't strike that guy. Amongst a group like that punching one person with a *bam!* would only result in a loss for me.

---

[1] Though Itoh Sensei said he changed the characters for the liberal politician 尾崎行雄 (1858 –1954) he did not. Served in the Japanese Diet for 63 years (1890–1953) and for his anti-militarism stance was jailed during both world wars. According to the Wikipedia article the father of the attacker "…later approached Ozaki to apologize in person for the actions of his son. Ozaki immediately responded with a 32-syllable *tanka* poem, which he handed to the surprised man:

If it was patriotism that drove the young man,

My would-be assassin deserves honor for it."

[2] 犬と猿の仲なる Mutual dislike (like dogs and monkeys apparently are in this expression).

[3] I presume Itoh Sensei is referring to a Kyudo style bow but it is unclear.

Anything other than making good use of the ensuing split second of indecision to make an escape would be a disaster. From there I laid about with the bow coupled with shouts of *Yaaa!* that coincided with bursting through the thick of fifteen or sixteen youths all bending back from my inertia to the left and right. Like a hero slashing a trail of blood to freedom, though I clearly recall inside my chest my heart was pounding. Less like a *Hichō* or flying bird and more like a *Hiton* or flying pig I ran free[1]. Here fully utilizing the moment while it lasted, I quickly threw the bow I had plundered at those seeking to fill in from the left and right the pathway I had opened. No shouted words accompanied this throw and I melted back into the throng.

My feeling at the time was that *I didn't understand myself.* The most frightening aspect being how dangerous my escape technique actually was. When it was all said and done I ended up with some measure of respect from the group of rascals, ever on the prowl for a confrontation. In fact the Flying Pig Boy became, against all odds, quasi-famous. This little scuffle too can well, only be seen as firmly I the grip of that which utilized the interval of one blink 『*Kibun Tenkan.*』 This has overall been a collection of both elite examples and small fry to be sure.

Insofar as is possible we have gathered together scenes of 『*Kibun Tenkan.*』 and 『*Chu-i Tenkan.*』 from here and there. I am not throwing these examples out as something that is applicable to only that particular situation or time, rather it is something that can be picked up again. It is akin to a single chain interlinked. I am of the belief that these will be of great use to those doing Shūgyō in 『*Gendai-teki Goshin Jutsu*』 as well as 『*Gendai-teki Shosei Jutsu.*』 Surely amongst my friends and readers there are those with similar experiences are not uncommon. From there one can infer what the Mabataku Ma no Hataraki is. And if that sketch can be formed then sending this document out into the world has not been for naught and the writer could not be more proud.

---

[1] 飛鳥 *Hichō*.　飛豚 Hiton.

其の六　　戰爭にも確かに忍術時代が來た

Chapter Six: With War Seemingly Certain,

The Era of Ninjutsu is Upon Us.[1]

Ninjutsu is not some group of lowborn, trivial techniques left over from a moldy era, but rather in this day and in this world, where everyone is half asleep or in a state of confusion, it is spinning and turning and twisting people about. As I previously took pains to explain, there is a 『*Goshin Jutsu*』 along with a 『*Shosei Jutsu.*』 that has been distilled from Ninjutsu that is matched with this day and time.

The rather decidedly unexpected reasoning behind this will be covered in addition to moving one level up and examining how far Ninjutsu has come from its origins. Further we will seek to understand, the width, breadth and depth of that territory that contains not a whiff of nonsense or trickery. Now in the grand scale of the spectacular wars between county and country, in one scene after another, Ninjutsu itself is playing an active role. Therefore discussing the fact that with war seemingly certain the era of Ninjutsu upon us is necessary. I must of course warn that delving into this particular issue with gusto was the original purpose of the author and that I intend to wrap it up with gusto.

Some five thousand odd years ago in China a grand schemer by the name of Shiyu[2] was using his might to cause pandemonium. It is said that he had a head as hard as copper blended with steel. Additionally it was said that through his magic he frequently caused thick fog to form. This murky figure, who so worried the Yellow Emperor[3], seems to have

---

[1] Published in 1937, so yeah. On July 7 The Marco Polo Bridge Incident, which was the start of Japanese forces invading China (often seen as the beginning of World War II in Asia).

[2] 蚩尤 Known in Chinese as *Chi You*, was a tribal leader of the ancient Nine Li 九黎 tribe. Famous as the tyrant who fought against the Yellow Emperor during the Three Sovereigns and Five Emperors Era 2852 BCE-2070 BCE.

[3] 黄帝 The Yellow Emperor. Tradition holds that he lived/reigned from 2697–2597BCE. He is later credited with being founder of the centralized state, a patron of esoteric arts, a cosmic ruler, and *a lord of the underworld*. Credited with numerous inventions and innovations

made use of Ninjutsu leading us to the conclusion he was something of a forefather to the art. The emperor crafted the *Shinan Sha[1]*, or south-facing chariot, a sort of chariot that utilizes magnets. Deploying this to find a true course he therefore was able to overcome the thick fog and destroy Shiyu.

Further in the Three Kingdoms Period[2] of China the famous tactician Komei Shokatsu[3] is also said to have made skillful use of fog during wartime. This leads us to believe that something similar to the Ninjutsu technique of Kiri-Gakure was being made use of in great fields of battle from way on back in the day.

In the European War cargo ships of the Triple Entente[4] sailing through the Mediterranean Sea beckoned attack by German submersibles. To counter this, a chemical filled *smoking box[5]* was

---

including (according to a 2nd Century Tomb inscription) "He devised upper and lower garments".

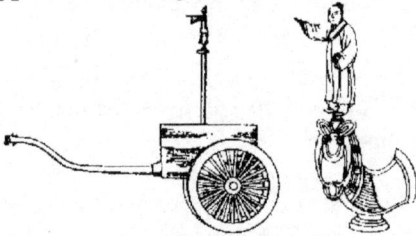

[1] 指南車 The south-pointing vehicle resembles a chariot with a movable pointer on top to indicate the direction, no matter which way the chariot turned. The pointer on the top was usually a human figure with an outstretched hand. There are no *Shinan Sha* still extant but they are frequently mentioned in ancient texts. Currently they are thought to not make use of magnets but rather a geared mechanism.

[2] 三国時代 Extending from 220 to 280 CE.

[3] 諸葛孔明 Chinese name: Zhuge Liang (181–234) Also known as Wolong 臥龍 or "Crouching Dragon". A chancellor of the state of Shu Han during the Three Kingdoms period. Often recognized as the greatest and most accomplished strategist of his era. Often depicted wearing a robe and holding a hand fan made of crane feathers.

[4] You should know this from middle school; you know the other side is the triple alliance.

[5] スモーキングボックス Rendered in Katakana.

attacked to the stern of the ship. Should a submersible chance to come into view, this device was pitched into the sea. Upon striking the water white smoke would begin to roil up and spread about a half mile in every direction this distraction was proved to enable craft to easily slip away. This is a correct use of the Kiri Gakure of Ninjutsu on such a large scale that it surely must be some world record. Further, adding even more *Kufū* [1] to this we have aircraft and so forth equipped with Enmaku or smoke screens in order to blind the enemy, which in itself is enough to astonish me. When it is all said and done it is clear that actual, refined battlefield applications of Kiri Gakure exist[2].

These days we have specialized military words like *Meisai*[3] or camouflage that serve as abbreviations for things like tents whose colouring is painted to match the earth around it. Or using the actual grass growing in the earth, or a drawing thereof to confuse aircraft seeking a sign of your presence. In addition, we have tanks and artillery batteries covered in grasses, military trains camouflaged and, like a stage set for a play, we have wooden tree shapes cut out of boards and painted so that the soldiers observing the movements of enemy troops can remain hidden. Everyone, clearly this is the borrowing of the Ninjutsu techniques of Moku Ton "Tree" escapes and Do Ton "Ground" Escapes for the battlefield. The uses of Moku Ton and Do Ton are used just as they were described in the previous chapters.

Perhaps the most surprising is the disruptive power of chemical light flares. These can serve to blind the enemy troops and can even burn them to death. Frequently new things like this emerge but the real issue lies in devising new *Kufu* to make the best use of these developments in the Ka Ton "Fire Escapes" of Ninjutsu.

---

[1] 工夫 Method of refinement. A trick or knack that enables you to do something, to carry out a technique despite adversity.
[2] There was in fact heavy use of submersibles by the Germans during The First World War in the Mediterranean, including the first submerged night attack. *"On 27th April 1915 the French armoured cruiser Léon Gambetta (12,500 tons) was hit at the mouth of the Adriatic in a submerged night attack with two torpedoes. The cruiser sank within 20 minutes, taking 648 men of its crew of 821 to the bottom of the Otranto Strait"*.   From uboat.net.
[3] 迷彩 Camouflage.

Other examples can be found in the *Hohei Souten[1]* or Infantry Manual from before the Russo-Japanese War. In it was written *"Should a grenade be thrown. Confirm it before taking cover."* However, those that lived through that terrifying experience relayed what they had learned and the *Souten* was rewritten and the meaning became *"Regardless of whether it has been confirmed or not, do not let down your guard, should a hand grenade land, in that same instant don't think but jump for cover."* This is a perfect example of how the *Gokui[2]* or essence of Ninjutsu can be applicable in these times. Further that 『*Shunkan Sayo*』 and 『*Mabataku no Ma no Hataraki*』 are perfectly matched, like the two parts of a *Waribashi[3]* that can be fitted back together. That in war the era of Ninjutsu has come causes us to realize many things from these few examples.

Well now beyond this we have the warning siren, the flack guns firing, fleeing from the rapid attack of the enemy aircraft and watching them peel away. The night sky appearing and disappearing as one slips into enemy territory to observe their movements. The aircraft that are blowing apart enemy cities or firebombing them all have a different task[4]. Each person is executing the one strike, one movement, one advance, one retreat of the Ninja[5]. Man and machine joined and each doing their task and enhancing the other. No, there is still more. The area that aircraft is flying in the big sky but the complete opposite of that is the battle occurring within the earth like a mole. The tunnel warfare, trench warfare are both battles of technicians competing against each other in Do Ton "Earth Escapes." Should we continue to delve deeper and deeper into the topic of war the field of Ninjutsu, which we are examining, will become confused so let's flip back to the distant past.

The Shichi-nin Sanada or Sanada's Seven, as they are known – in reality unmistakably including the great masters Sasuke Sarutobi and Saizou Kirikagure – lead by the Strategist cum Ninja Yukimura Sanada who used numerous decoys of himself on the battlefield. This Jin Ton "Human Escapes" frequently resulted in confusion among his enemies and the technique has come to be known by strategists in China and

---

[1] 歩兵操典

[2] 極意 Essence or mystery.

[3] 割り箸 Disposable chopsticks made of wood or bamboo.

[4] Quite the spooky foreshadowing here...

[5] 一擧一動一進一退 Ikko Ichi Do Isshin Ittai

Europe[1]. The likes of Sho Kai Seki[2] and Cho Gaku Ryo[3] and numerous others come and go. Hitlers and Mussolinis appear here and there and are gone just as quickly, we can hardly postulate the theory that

---

[1] So this refers to "The Seven Spears of Ueda" 上田七本槍 who played a pivotal role in the battle of Ueda Castle in the fifth year of Keicho 慶長 5 年 (1600 年) just before the battle of Sekigahara 関ヶ原の戦い. Tokugawa Hidetada 徳川秀忠 had surrounded Sanada Masayuki 真田昌 幸 at Ueda Castle. At some point during the   siege seven peasants left the castle ostensibly to harvest some wheat. The enemy, seeing an easy target attacked with numerous mounted men. The "peasants" turned out to be seasoned warriors (and in some accounts were actually the famous Ninja mentioned). The warriors were eventually even praised by the Shogun Tokugawa.

[2] 蒋介石 The Japanese reading of Chiang Kai-shek (1887 –1975). President of the Republic of China and later Taiwan. Studied at the Tokyo Shinbu Gakko (東京振武學校), an Imperial Japanese Army Academy Preparatory School for Chinese students, in 1907. After the Japanese invasion of Manchuria in 1931, Chiang adopted the slogan "*first internal pacification, then external resistance*" detailing his plan to first rid China of the communists, then the Japanese.

[3] 張学良 In Chinese: Zhang Xueliang (1901- 2001). Ruler of Manchuria and much of northern China after the assassination of his father, Zhang Zuolin, by the Japanese in 1928. The Japanese believed that Zhang who was known as a womanizer and an opium addict, would be susseptable to Japanese influence. Later however he decided to rid his command of Japanese influence by having two prominent pro-Tokyo officials executed in front of the assembled guests at a dinner party in January 1929. In the Xi'an incident (12 December 1936), Zhang and another general Yang Hucheng kidnapped Chiang Kai-shek and imprisoned the head of the Kuomintang government until he agreed to form a united front with the Communists against the Japanese invasion. After the negotiations, Chiang agreed to unite with the Communists and drive the Japanese out of China. When Chiang was released, Zhang chose to return to the capital with him. However, once they were away from Zhang's loyal troops, Chiang had him put under house arrest, where he remained under a loose house arrest for the next 40 years. Wikipedia.

"They won't come here."

The fundamental applications of Ninjutsu for the modern world are gradually increasing beyond the level of what they were in the past. Further, more so than *now* they are showing a tendency to increase from *now on*. This may seem to be mysterious but in reality there are numerous un-mysterious points for the eye to fix on. For this reason it must be stated that it is the most effective method in operation today. In fact Ninjutsu-style 「*Goshin Jutsu*」 and 「*Shosei Jutsu*」 had no choice but to come about. And of course we have Gingetsu Itoh who comes in like a whirl of wind from one direction then another like some kind of aged whorl of hair [dust devil] wriggling its way out a problem that can be dealt with at ones leisure and you don't have to be exposed to me. Before we can get to that let us end the now completed S h i n Gata Ninjutsu [The entirely New Essence of Ninjutsu] Gokui.

ABOUT THE AUTHOR
伊藤銀月

Gingetsu Itoh (1871-1944)
Author and Commentator

Itoh Sensei was born 伊藤銀二 Itoh Ginji on October 21st in the Fourth Year of the Meiji Emperor. A reporter for the 萬朝報 *Yorozu Morning Paper*, Itoh Sensei became known for his original style and anti-modernist stance. He published a critique of civilization with *Poetic Tokyo* 詩的東京 as well as a long novel *Esthetics of a Small Society* 美的小社会 in addition to the history books *The History of the Japanese People* 日本民族史 and *The History of Surprising Words* 日本警語史. He died in the Nineteenth Year of the Showa Era at age 73.

Gingetsu Itoh wrote four books on Ninjutsu.

1. *Ninjutsu to Yojutsu 1909

2. *Ninjutsu no Gokui 1917

3. Ninjutsu to Kankin Jutsu 1922

4. *Gendaijin no Ninjutsu 1937

* These books have been translated

ABOUT THE TRANSLATOR

eric shahan has been living, studying Japanese and training Kobudo under the Jinenkan banner since he moved to Japan more than a decade ago. This is the third book by Itoh Sensei he has translated.

ABOUT THE EDITOR

Linda Lawler Shahan is the mother of the translator and is wondering when he will come for a visit... and for how long.

Printed in Dunstable, United Kingdom

64367101R00117